1 MONTH OF
FREE
READING

at
www.ForgottenBooks.com

By purchasing this book you are eligible for one month membership to ForgottenBooks.com, giving you unlimited access to our entire collection of over 1,000,000 titles via our web site and mobile apps.

To claim your free month visit:

www.forgottenbooks.com/free911145

ISBN 978-0-266-92816-4
PIBN 10911145

VISITORS'
ILLUSTRATED
GUIDE
TO
BOMBAY.

BY D. A. PINDER.

—

WITH MAPS.

—

Bombay:

G. CLARIDGE & Co.,

CAXTON PRINTING WORKS, MARINE STREET

1904

—

preface.

————————

FEW words of preface seem called for in the circumstances under which this little work is issued. It does not presume to the dignity of a history, but seeks simply to act the humbler part of a guide, recalling the more important incidents from the records of the city of Bombay and pointing out *en passant* the most salient features of interest.

The present edition has been considerably enlarged and further embellished with a series of views reproduced from photographs, and with its fund of general information, its Maps, and portable form, will, it is hoped, prove a useful companion to the visitor.

The plan followed has been to divide the city into several districts and under the heading of a "Round-about Ramble" to conduct the sightseer through localities which embrace (1) The Esplanade and Fort, (2) Colaba, (3) Malabar Hill, (4) Byculla and Mazagon, and (5) Parel and the northern suburbs of the island, each journey being complete in itself.

The guide is prefaced by a brief history of the city and supplemented by other information descriptive of the most important "Places of Interest" in the vicinity of the capital of the Bombay Presidency.

Index.

●●●●●●●●●●●●

BOMBAY—PAST AND PRESENT.

A Round-about Ramble.

THE ESPLANADE AND FORT.

Index.

COLABA.

MALABAR HILL.

Index.

A Glance at Bombay's Past.

THE territories comprised within the boundaries of the Indian Peninsula, and especially the districts of the Bombay Presidency, are richly crowded with places of antiquarian, archæological, and historical interest ; yet none surpass either in these aspects or in natural picturesqueness, beauty, and salubrity of situation, the city of Bombay—the Capital of the Western Presidency. Situated in lat. 18° 53′ 45″ and long 72° 52′, the island of Bombay may be described as being almost surrounded by water. Its western shores are washed by the Indian Ocean, the waters of which go to form the magnificent harbour on the eastern side of the city. The island, which is about ten miles in length, from Colaba in the south to Mahim and Sion in the North, is of irregular shape, and, with the exception of Malabar and Cumballa Hills, the former being about 180 feet in height, is but a few feet above sea level. The commercial city proper, as separated from the native town and suburbs, is located on the narrow point of land

to the north of Colaba, and although the ancient walls
have long since been razed to the ground is still known
as the Fort, while the principal public buildings occupy
sites on the adjoining Esplanade, many of them having
been built on land reclaimed from the sea on the Back
Bay side of the island. The city, which has during
recent years been appropriately called "Bombay the
Beautiful," possesses natural advantages both as a place
of residence and for defence that must have in former
years singled it out as a favourable site for habitation.
The earlier records of its history are somewhat buried
in obscurity, for although previous to the tenth century
it is stated to have been called by the natives "Mahim,"
it was not until the latter period that its present title
" Bombay," was first mentioned historically.

In giving a brief summary of the most important
events that have transpired during the past five hundred
years, it may be as well to mention that Bombay was
first occupied by Europeans in 1332, a Portuguese force
having in that year captured the islands, which two years
later was, with the neighbouring islands of Salsette and
Bassein, ceded to them by the King of Gujerat. Early
in the seventeenth century a treaty was entered into
between the English and Portuguese, which allowed the
former to trade at Bombay, and in 1661 the island was
ceded to the British as part of the dowry of the Infanta
Catherina on her marriage with Charles II., the treaty
specifying that the gift was for the better improvement
of English interest and commerce in the East Indies.
The Earl of Marlborough and Sir Abraham Shipmen,
with five men-of-war and five hundred soldiers, arrived

two years later to take over formal possession, but difficulties arose in connection with the negotiations, with the result that King Charles did not have complete control of the island till about 1664. The population at that time was only some 10,000 souls, and the yearly revenue a very little over £6,000, and the King, after the lapse of a few years, finding the acquisition unprofitable, handed it over to the East India Company "on payment of an annual rental of £10." The Commissioners deputed to take over the island arrived in the Company's ship "Constantinople Merchant" and gave the following interesting details in their account of the ceremony which took place on the 23rd September, 1668 :—"At our landing we were mett by Governor Gary, etc., Officers who at the head of their several Companys military drawne up, by the sea side received us with very much respect and ceremony ; and soe accompanyed us in to the Fort ; where Governor Gary caused all the soldiers to make their approach toward us in military order, first being by the Cheife Officers commanded to lay downe their armes, and to march towards us without them, yet in decent Ranke, and there in the head of them all he he made a short speech, much to the honour and praise of the Honble Company and caused his Majesty's Privy Seale to be publiquely read. At which the officers and soldiers for the generality were well pleased, that his Majesty had disposed the Island to the Honble Companys to whom they own'd obedient. After which we cause the Company's Commission to the President and Council, together with your Commission to us to be also reac publiquely, which being done they marched back to thei

armes, and tooke them up for the Honble Company
when John Goodier made a short speech to encourage
and confirm them in their obedience, by assuring every
man his former quality and pay. The several Officers
were very instrumental in their several degrees and
stations to promote our desires, and further the Company's Interest, when divers soldiers deserted their
service, and with their mutinous example had like to
have infected many more, who layed downe their Armes,
denying any future service, wherefore we were enforced
to confine them in a room, in order to sending them on
bord, which when they saw they used the mediations of
Captain Toldery, that they might be admitted to their
armes again, promising much obedience for the future they
were received accordingly, only lost this by their re-
fractoriness, that civility and kindness we intended to
shew them, we are now enforced to exchange for a more
reserved demeanour."

Following the taking over of the Island the Company
made liberal provisions for the defence of the town and
for the encouragement of trade, with the result that on
Dr. John Fryer paying a visit in 1675, he found the
population had increased to 60,000 persons, and in a
description of Bombay stated that 120 pieces of ordnance
were mounted within the Castle, and in alluding to the
present Fort District, which comprises the locality now
bounded by Rampart Row, Esplanade and Hornby
Roads, and Fort Street, describes the then town as being
a mile in length, the houses, with the exception of those
left by the Portuguese and some built by the Company,
as being low and thatched with leaves. The Custom

ESPLANADE ROAD AND FLORAL FOUNTAIN.

House and warehouses were tiled, oystershells being used in the windows instead of glass. There was also a reasonably handsome bazaar at one end of the town looking into a field where cows and buffaloes grazed.

About this period the Portuguese and Mahrattas gave considerable trouble to the English. In 1688 the Sidee Admiral of the Great Mogal captured Mazagon, and afterwards laid siege to Bombay Castle, but the English eventually persuaded the Mogal Emperor to get his Admiral to withdraw his forces to the north of the Island. In 1721 the Mahratta chief Angria and the Portuguese gave further trouble, fired on Mahim Fort, and built a battery at Coorla. Tanna in 1739 was captured from the latter by the Mahrattas, and in 1756 Angria's strongholds to the south of Bombay were captured by the English, the pirate chief being taken prisoner by Admiral Watson and Colonel Clive. Towards the close of the eighteenth century Bombay despatched several expeditions against the Mahrattas, sanguinary engagements taking place at Tanna, Kalyan, Wurgaum, and Bassein, and resulting in à treaty that gave the British possession of Salsette, Elephanta, Karanja, and Hog Islands, in exchange for Bassein, the English outposts being advanced to Tanna. About the beginning of the last century Bombay furnished troops for the various campaigns in Mysore and the south, the local army at that time consisting of three European and nine Native Regiments. General Wellesley, writing in 1804, alluding to the defencelessness of the city, declined to send away the 84th European Regiment, as it was the only one left in garrison, and, in view of probable combination of the French and

Dutch Indian squadrons, considered the defensive force of Bombay ought not to be weakened too much. Military operations followed against Holkar and other chiefs, and in 1817 the battle of Kirkee resulted in the flight of the Peshwa and occupation of Poona, Khandesh being acquired the following year, and the Sattara Kingdom annexed in 1848, the Province of Scinde having been conquered in 1843 by a force under Sir C. Napier. The Mutiny year, 1857, passed fairly quietly in so far as the Bombay army was concerned, but an officer and a private of a local native regiment having been detected formulating treason were in that year blown from the guns on the Esplanade.

The Great Indian Peninsula Railway, the first line constructed in the Presidency, was opened to Tanna in 1853, the Bombay, Baroda and Central Indian Railway entering the city in 1864. On the opening of the Suez Canal, the P. & O. Company took up the contract for a weekly mail service to Europe, a monthly service *via* the Persian Gulf having first been inaugurated in 1798, the postage rate by the latter service then being: For each letter Rs. 10 per ¼ tola, Rs. 15 per ½ tola, and Rs. 20 per tola.

Bombay's latter history partakes wholly of a pacific and prosperous character. Its extension has been steady though slow, and great improvements have in course of years been made in the condition of its streets, markets, and public edifices. The visitor need not think he is wasting time, however long he tarries in the city. It is one of the most remarkable as well as one of the largest and liveliest cities on the earth, its " native town " in some respects being the most characteristic to be seen in India. The new public buildings are magnificent, nature everywhere enhancing their architectural beauty. The view from Malabar Hill, covered with commodious bungalows and rich gardens—the dark hills making a background to the sparkling blue of the Indian Ocean, and to the shipping beyond Colaba—extends over as fair prospect as Asia can furnish. Its spacious markets are cleaner and better arranged than any others in the British Empire ; its Victoria Terminus is a sumptuous Palace of Travel, and, whatever faults may be found with the various styles adopted by official designers, the general effect of the groups of buildings between the Fort and Malabar Hill is certainly good. These labours, which have transformed Bombay from a fishing village to the virtual Metropolis of India, can only be judged by those who remember the place in the days of the great Mutiny. Where are now seen clean and broad roads green maidans, stately groves of trees, spires, towers, and imposing facades, was half a century ago an unfavourable foreshore extended from Colaba northwards. Once settled at an hotel or in the house of some friend, the stranger will doubtless become familiar with the handsome buildings, such as the Sailors' Home, the new Secretariat, the University Hall and Rajabai Clock Tower, the High Court, Public Works Offices, Post and Telegraph Offices, Statue of the Queen-Empress, and the Terminus of the G. I. P. Railway ; but the native city and its population are really, however, the most interesting feature of Bombay, and to see it at its best the visitor should take an early morning stroll in the Crawford

Markets or a drive in the evening through Abdul Rahman Street.

The triangle between that street and the Carnac and Kalbadevi Roads contains an epitome of the whole peninsula, and a good portion of its wealth. The Mahomedans live chiefly along the south of the Parel Road, and the Parsees at Dhobee Talao. Endless are the mosques, temples, and shrines, and fire temples, and ceaseless the flood of varied Asiatic life hereabouts, not sombre in colour like a European crowd but gay in many colours. And when the visitor passes along Kennedy Sea Face he will find on Malabar Hill a European suburb, once a wild, rocky jungle of scrub and snake dens, but to-day a cultured paradise of verdure and luxurious living. From the Ridge, or the Ladies' Gymkhana, the view of the splendid city, with its buildings, harbour, and its hills, cannot be surpassed.

The Municipal history of Bombay is of comparatively recent date. Previous to 1872 civic affairs were conducted by a Commissioner and a Bench of Justices, but in the latter year the Municipal Bill received the sanction of Government, the first elections taking place in 1873. A new Act came into force in 1888 by which it was laid down that the Municipal Corporation should consist of seventy-two members, sixteen of whom are nominated by Government, sixteen by the Bench of Justices, two by the University, two by the Chamber of Commerce, and thirty-six elected by the ratepayers at the ward elections, for a period of three years. The Standing Committee consists of twelve members, four nominated by Government and the remainder elected by the

PART OF THE FORT.

Corporation, each body annually electing its own chairman. The principal executive officer is the Commissioner, who is aided by a strong and well-paid staff of Health Officers and Engineers.

Bombay is rapidly becoming a first-class manufacturing town. The total number of spinning and weaving mills working and in course of erection numbering eighty, containing 25,33,382 spindles, in addition to 23,125 looms, and employing a daily average of 86,913 hands ; the yearly consumption of cotton averaging 4,93,114 candies. There are also a few silk factories and numerous iron foundries and workshops. The valuable foreshore properties on the harbour side of the city are administered by the Port Trust, the board of which consists of members nominated by Government, the Chamber of Commerce, and the public. The revenues of the Trust amount annually to about fifty lakhs of rupees.

On lands owned by the Bombay Port Trust and Bombay Improvement Trust there has during the past few years been erected a large number of handsome buildings, mainly set apart for residences for Europeans. The whole of the area lying to the eastward of Colaba Causeway and covering land between the Sailors' Home and Grant Buildings, has now practically been covered with a number of four and five storey dwellings, many of which are well designed, and afford accommodation for a large number of European families. The whole of the estate on which these flats and buildings have been erected belongs to the Port Trust, who also own large areas of land on the harbour side of the island. Near

the Ballard Pier the Trustees have recently reclaimed a
good deal of land and laid out broad roads upon it, and
propose making further improvements at this point,
where a new dock, 2,600 feet in length is to be built, together with a wharf alongside which the Mail Steamers
will be able to land passengers.

The works for the defence of the harbour and city
from attack by sea consist of three well constructed land
forts situated at Colaba, Malabar Hill, and Mahaluxmi,
and three harbour Forts, namely, Oyster Rock (off
Colaba), Middle Ground (off the Apollo Bunder), and
Cross Island (off the Prince's Dock). All these Forts
are armed with 10-inch R.M.L., 10-inch R.B.L., 6-inch
R.B.L. guns, and in addition are protected by quick-
firing and machine guns. The above defences are
supplemented by the vessels of the Royal Navy. The
force comprising the military garrison consists of three
companies European garrison artillery, one British infantry regiment, two native infantry regiments, two
sections of sub-marine miners, the Light Horse, Artillery
and Rifle Volunteers, and the head quarters companies
of the Great Indian Peninsular Railway and Bombay,
Baroda and Central India Railway Volunteers.

A Round About Ramble.

The Esplanade and Fort.

THE visitor desirous of seeing the most important places of interest within the neighbourhood of the Esplanade, and what is still known as the Fort, should select as his starting point the WELLINGTON FOUNTAIN, which will be found at the south end of the Esplanade Road, and in close proximity to the principal hotels of the city. The fountain which occupies a commanding position in the centre of the open space facing the Sailors' Home, was erected by public subscription to the memory of the Duke of Wellington.

The ROYAL ALFRED SAILORS' HOME, which occupies one of the finest sites in the city at the top of the Apollo Bunder Road, was erected at a cost of Rs. 3,66,629. Its construction was commenced in 1872 and finished four years later, when Lord Lytton, then Viceroy of India, opened the Home. Towards the cost of construc-

tion H. H. Khunderao, Gaekwar of Baroda, contributed
Rs. 2,00,000 in commemoration of the visit of H.R.H.
the Duke of Edinburgh, by whom the foundation-stone
was originally laid in a less conspicuous position on the
Hornby Road, from which place it was afterwards removed to its present site. The building has a frontage of
270 feet, and is 55 feet in breadth, having two wings,
that on the north being 114 feet and that on the south
58 feet in length. A medallion of the Gaekwar is placed
over the entrance porch. The Home, which is faced
with blue basalt, is built with Porbunder, Coorla, and
Hemnagar stone, and is embellished with carvings and
sculpture, that on the front gable representing Neptune
with nymphs and seahorses. There is a library and bar
for the use of the inmates, the dining-room and dormitories being large and lofty. Its objects are to provide seamen frequenting the port with board and lodging at a
moderate charge; to protect them from imposition and ex-
tortion ; to encourage them to husband their hardearned
wages, and to provide them, through the Superintendent of the Home, with a safe depository for their savings
and a medium of remitting the same with security to their
friends at home ; to promote their moral, intellectual,
and professional improvement, and to afford them the
opportunity of religious instruction. The Home, which
is conducted on principles of order, comfort, and liberality, is also a refuge for the shipwrecked and distressed
mariner.

Passing down the Bunder Road, to the east of the
Sailors' Home will be found the well-arranged stables of
the BOMBAY POSTAL DEPARTMENT, situated at the

YACHT CLUB.

SAILORS' HOME.

end of a short lane to the left, near which the visitor will observe a block of buildings known as the ESPLANADE HOTEL ANNEXE, erected in the Elizabethan style.

In the block of buildings on the right of the road are the RIPON and VOLUNTEER ARTILLERY CLUBS. The " Ripon, " which is the leading Parsee Club in the city, was called after the late Viceroy of that name, and is managed on the same basis as the principal European clubs. The rooms are attractively furnished and well adapted to the requirements of the members.

Situated in well laid out grounds and occupying a prominent position on the harbour frontage, are the buildings of the ROYAL BOMBAY YACHT CLUB, which consist of two blocks, one on either side of the roadway, that to the visitor's left being the club house proper, and the lofty one on the right the residential chambers. The former building has been considerably enlarged in recent years. It is in the domestic Gothic style, costing originally about Rs. 36,000, and is a light and elegant structure, consisting of timber framing filled in with red brickwork and having at its south-east corner a lofty look-out tower. The billiard-room and offices are on the ground floor, and on the floor above, approached by a broad staircase, is a spacious dining hall, 55 feet by 30 feet, and a large ball room. The club house also contains cloak, reading, and dressing rooms, and is situated in spacious grounds that are well laid out. The building and grounds are lighted by electricity and from the balconies or the promenade on the harbour side a splendid view can be obtained over the waterway. Military bands play on the promenade during certain

evenings in the week, and in addition to frequent dances
during the season, a club regatta and aquatic sports take
place off the bunder during February. The visitor will
next arrive at the head of the bunder..

The APOLLO BUNDER or Wellington Pier is said to
have derived its name from a corruption of the word
pallow (a fish), and though it bears on its eastern face
the inscription " Wellington Pier," the latter designation is now seldom if ever used. The Apollo Bunder
apparently dates from about the year 1820, but since
then it has been lengthened and enlarged at considerable
expense, so that at the present time, and especially
during the fair season, when the military bands play in
the adjoining Yacht Club compound, from 6 P.M. to
7-30 P. M., it is one of the favourite resorts for Europeans,
the roadway on those evenings being crowded with
carriages and the promenade round the bunder head
thronged with pedestrians. The view obtainable over
the harbour from the latter point is one of the finest
seascapes in the world, and with the shipping and the
middle ground battery in the foreground, and Butcher's
Island (where the Submarine Miners are stationed),
Elephanta, Karanja, and the Ghauts in the background,
make up a picture that will long be remembered for its
beauty, either viewed during the heat of the day when
the sun plays on the water with dazzling brilliancy,
when the sun is setting and giving a pleasing effect of
light and shade, or when seen by moonlight. The
Bunder has been aptly called the " Gate of Western
India, " and, previous to the opening of the Ballard Pier
was, in the fair season, the place where most of the

new arrivals by sea were landed. The title is still not inappropriate, for the scene at the pier head on the arrival or departure of the P. & O. mail steamers is one of much bustle and excitement, as the postal mails are still landed there, and it has for long past been the place where Viceroys, Governors, and other distinguished persons have arrived or departed.

The passenger pavilion at the head of the Bunder is in the Burmese style of architecture, the pagoda-shaped roof, which is supported on twenty-four columns, being 34 feet above the ground level. The pavilion is 100 feet in length, is ornamented with open carvings, in which the monogram of the Port Trust is artistically worked, and forms a convenient shelter for persons awaiting the arrival or departure of boats. At the north-east corner of the Bunder is a small octagonal structure containing a machine for registering the rise and fall of the tides, and close by, on the right hand side of the road leading from the pier head, is another small building in which are located the Postal, Customs, and Police Offices. Passing round the harbour face of the pier and proceeding westward towards the Lansdowne Road, the APOLLO BUNDER RESTAURANT, under Messrs. Green & Co.'s management, will be noticed. A room is set apart for the use of ladies at the east end of the building, and overhead a good view of the harbour can be obtained from the balcony of the dining room.

THE TAJ MAHAL HOTEL, which occupies a large area of land at this point is one of the most spacious and attractive buildings erected in the city and as an hotel is one of the finest to be found in the East. It possesses many pleasing architectural features and is surmounted by a lofty central tower. The interior arrangements are in every way worthy of the city, the decoration of the large dining hall, the billiard and other public rooms having been carried out with great taste. The hotel can accommodate over three hundred residents.

The various residential blocks to the south and west of the hotel have all been built during recent years and are tenanted for the most part by Europeans. On the left of the Lansdowne Road is the BOWEN MEMORIAL CHURCH, the foundation stone of which was laid by Bishop Thorburn. Services are held in the room on the ground floor on Sundays at 11 A.M. and 6 P.M., the upper floor being set apart for the residence of the Minister. The three separate buildings comprising the APOLLO HOTEL are located at the top of the road, and have a commanding frontage on Colaba Causeway. The hotel consists of about one hundred separate suites of rooms.

Opposite the hotel are the rooms of the YOUNG MEN'S CHRISTIAN ASSOCIATION. The building was erected on land given by Government, and consists of a room set apart for lectures and religious services, a reading room and drawing room for members, containing the Macpherson Library, and a reading and coffee room open to all comers. There are spacious verandahs round the building. In rear of the rooms, which stand in a neat garden, are tennis courts, an Athletic Club, which embraces cricket and other games, being connected with the institution, which has branch rooms at Grant Road. The objects of

BOMBAY CASTLE FROM THE HARBOUR.

this Association are to promote the spiritual improvement and general welfare of young men of all classes. The Association is unsectarian, and is managed by a committee of representatives from the different Evangelical Churches of Bombay.

Leaving the above rooms on his left and the fountain on his right, the visitor will then enter the MAYO ROAD, on the left of which will be noticed the YOUNG WOMEN'S CHRISTIAN ASSOCIATION Building in which accommodation is provided for a large number of the members who are engaged in business in the city. There is a large lecture hall on the ground floor as well as reception and other rooms, all well arranged for the comfort of the residents. Proceeding down the roadway the next object of interest is the BANDSTAND, an octagonal structure built of wood and iron, and said to be erected on the site of the first European Cemetery. Military Bands play here on certain evenings, the circle round the stand forming a capital promenade. From this point an extensive view can be obtained over the piece of water known as BACK BAY, which is enclosed between Colaba Point on the south and Malabar Hill on the north. The greater portion of the land along the foreshore of the bay, on which has been constructed the B. B. & C. I. Railway line and the Queen's Road (the latter thoroughfare being opened in 1870 on the occasion of the visit of the Duke of Edinburgh) was reclaimed in former years and converted into pleasant rides, open spaces, or sites for handsome buildings. Glancing towards the south the stranger will see the PRONG'S LIGHTHOUSE and the spire of ST. JOHN'S CHURCH towering over the barracks at Colaba,

B

and in the middle distance the tower of the PARSEE
SANITARIUM, the Railway Terminus, and Wodehouse
Bridge. From the bridge to the foot of MALABAR HILL,
the KENNEDY SEA FACE forms a good ride for equestrians
and skirts the bay, following the line of which to the
right will be seen among the trees the WILSON COLLEGE
and the rising ground of MALABAR HILL, where a large
number of Europeans reside, and at the extreme point
of which is GOVERNMENT HOUSE.

Almost opposite the Bandstand is the SWIMMING
BATH, owned by the Back Bay Swimming Bath
Company, Limited. The BATH which is about 100 feet
long, is open from 6 A.M. to 6 P.M. on week days, and
from 6 A.M. to 1 P.M. on Sundays and holidays. Admission,
As. 4. The Back Bay Baths are reserved for ladies on
Tuesdays and Saturdays, from 10 A.M. to 1 P. M. Close to
the above is the Victoria Baths which are set apart for
the use of Parsees.

Passing the statue of the late Mr. Sorabjee S. Bengallee
and following the Mayo Road from the Bandstand in a
northern direction, on the left will be noticed the railed-
in piece of ground known as the OVAL or Rotten Row,
which forms a capital ride for equestrians, and is one
mile in circumference.

On his right hand the visitor will doubtless be
impressed by the fine range of buildings that line the
roadway, the first of which is the SECRETARIAT. The
building is 443 feet in length, having at each end wings
81 feet in breadth. It consists of four floors, and was
completed in March 1874, at a cost of Rs. 12,60,844.
It has a fine entrance hall on the west side, the main

staircase communicating direct with the upper floors, the rooms on which, with the exception of the Council Hall and Library, are very small and inconvenient, the exterior appearance of the edifice as seem from Back Bay being far from attractive. The main centre of the building is provided with arcaded verandahs on the west or front, the remaining portion of the frontage up to the wings being retired and protected by sun shades, supported on brackets and corbels. On the east side closed communication corridors run throughout the building. The north faces of the wings are arcaded, the south corridors being enclosed. The Council Hall, Library and Committee-rooms are on the first floor.

Crossing over the end of Fuller Road, the stranger will next approach the well laid out University Gardens, one of the prettiest open spaces in the city, in which are situated the handsome buildings known as the Sir Cowasjee Jehangir or University Hall, and the Rajabai Tower and Library.

The UNIVERSITY HALL, which is the building to the south of the Gardens, is, so far as architectural design goes one of the most elegant on the Esplanade. It is in the French style, was erected from the designs of the late Sir Gilbert Scott; cost Rs. 3,79,389, and was completed in 1874. The hall, in which meetings of the Senate take place, is 104 feet in length, has a breadth of 44 feet, the extreme height of the roof being 63 feet from the Minton tiled floor. Entering by the doorway under the porch at the north end, the building will be seen to be provided with a gallery round three sides, supported on ornamental iron brackets. The several windows are filled with stained glass, those at the side containing the arms of past Chancellors of the University. Several chandeliers are suspended from the roof, while at the south end is a raised dais for the Chancellor, surrounded by seats, the body of the hall being provided with ornamental cane seated benches. On the outside of the Senate Hall open staircases lead from the verandah to the gallery inside the building, the exterior design of which reflects great credit on the architect. The executive government of the University is vested in the Syndicate consisting of the Vice-Chancellor and eight of the Fellows, who are elected annually by the several Faculties. Towards the cost of the building the late Sir Cowasjee Jehangir contributed Rs. 1,00,000, a statue of the Parsee knight being placed in the Gardens outside the main porch, while on the east side of the hall is another statue erected to Sir Thomas Ormiston, the designer of the Prince's and Victoria Docks and the Prongs Lighthouse.

The RAJABAI TOWER and the UNIVERSITY LIBRARY were also designed by Sir Gilbert Scott, the total length of the Library building being 152 feet ; having an open arcade running along its west front, with staircases at either end leading to the floor above, which consists of one spacious room, 146 feet, by 30 feet, containing the library. Over the carriage porch is the Rajabai Tower, which forms such a conspicuous feature in the city. and which is 280 feet in height. The tower is ornamented with 24 large stone figures representing the various castes of Western India. The clock face, which is 167 feet from the ground, is over 16 feet in diameter, the clock being

RAJABAI TOWER.

provided with a set of chimes which play daily at 6 A.M., 1-30 P.M., 5 P.M., and 9 P.M. There are sixteen bells in the clock, arranged in a couple of tiers, the eight smaller bells forming the upper tier and the eight larger bells the lower. The machinery is of a compound character, one part being for the chiming of the quarters and striking the hours, and the other for playing the tunes. The entire cost of the Library and Tower, namely, Rs. 5,47,703, being defrayed by the gift of Premchund Roychund, Esq. Permission to ascend the tower should be obtained from the Registrar of the University. In 1891 two young Parsee females fell from the upper balcony of the tower to the ground, a distance of 260 feet, and met with an almost instantaneous death.

Leaving the Gardens and proceeding further along the Mayo Road, the next building is the HIGH COURT, a massive and somewhat sombre looking structure designed by Colonel Fuller, R. E., and completed at a cost of Rs. 16,44,528. It is built in the Gothic style and is some 560 feet in length, 187 in breadth ; the highest point of the roof being 178 feet from the ground, The Judges have private staircases on the west, the entrance for the general public being on the east or Eldon Road side. A fine main staircase leads to the upper floors. The Criminal Sessions Court is on the second floor, where three Appellate and three Original Courts and the Law Library with its valuable collection of legal books are also located. The decorations of the Sessions Court are in cream and gold, this Court containing two full length portraits one of Sir John Peter Grant, Puisne Judge, 1828-70, subscribed for by the people of Bombay in the latter year.   The sessions are held during February, April, June, September, and November. The office of the Administrator-General is on the third floor ; those of the Sheriff of Bombay, Clerk of the Crown, Insolvency Court, and the Registrars of Births Marriages, and Deaths and of Public Companies on the ground floor.

The next building to the north of the High Court is the one in which the offices of the PUBLIC WORKS DEPARTMENT are located.   The building, facing Church Gate Street, which is in the Venetian Gothic style was erected from designs by Colonel H. St. Clair Wilkins, R. E.   The work, which was commenced on the 21st May, 1869, was carried out under the orders of Lieut-Col. J. A. Fuller, R.E., and J. H. E. Hart, C. E., and was completed in April, 1892, at a cost of Rs. 4,14,484, or some Rs. 24,000 under the amount sanctioned by Government.   The main building, which is nearly 300 feet in length by 50 feet breadth, consists of two storeys and a ground floor, with the addition of a third storey over the centre portion, the highest point of the roof being about 176 feet from the ground level.   In 1894 the west wing was added on the Mayo Road side.

To the left of Mayo Road are the statues of Sir Richard Temple, Lord Reay and Lord Sandhurst the former having been Governor of Bombay from 1877 to 1880, the second from 1885 to 1890 and the latter fulfilling a similar office from 1895 to 1900.

At the far end of Church Gate Street are the ADMINISTRATIVE OFFICES OF THE BOMBAY, BARODA AND CENTRAL INDIA RAILWAY COMPANY, which were design-

ed by the late Mr. F. W. Stevens. They occupy a site on
the piece of ground at the south end of Marine Lines,
directly opposite Church Gate Station. The style chosen
is early Gothic with an Oriental feeling, and is similar in
character and detail to the adjacent public buildings, a
condition laid down by the Government. The building
is faced with coursed blue basalt stone, and the domes,
mouldings, cornices, enrichments, etc., are in Porebunder
stone. The length of the west *facade* is 280 feet, and
with its domes and imposing central tower gives a most
effective appearance. The buildings consists of three
floors for office purposes, but in the centre there is an
extra floor for records, etc. On the ground floor accom
modation is provided for the Traffic, Police, Medical, and
Cashier's Departments, and this, ike all the other floors,
has a fine verandah all round the building. Projecting
out from the centre of the west *facade* is a handsome
carriage porch for general use, and on the south side is
a similar porch, but not so large, for the use of the Agent
and heads of departments. From the hall on the ground
floor, an hydraulic lift is provided for the convenience of
passengers. On the first floor accommodation is provided
for the Agent's and Engineering Departments, as also a
spacious Board-room in the centre of the bnilding. The
second floor is occupied by the Audit Department and
Government Examiner of Accounts. The tower is 160
feet in height above ground level, and has an imposing
appearance from all parts of the Esplanade. The base
of the tower is square and is continued upwards in this
form to 100 feet above the ground ; it than takes the
form of an octagon, than a circular form, crowned with

a masonry dome. The rooms in the tower are utilized for storing records and for the large water tanks for the fire-service and for working the hydraulic lift. The central gable of the west *facade* is crowned by a fine piece of sculpture typical of " Engineering. " The garden is well laid out and is divided from the public road by railings. The estimated cost of the building was 7½ lakhs of rupees,

GENERAL POST OFFICE : Facing the Public Works building and occupying a good site on the opposite side of Church Gate Street is the General Post Office, which was completed in 1872 at a cost of Rs. 5,94,200. Inside the central hall on the ground floor are enclosures for the sale of stamps, etc., while on either side of the hall are places for the registration or insurance of letters, a *poste restante* and an enquiry office. The Parcel Post, Money Order, and Saving Bank Departments are on the first floor. Plans for a more commodious office, near the Victoria Terminus, have recently been prepared.

The *Post Restante* is open as follows :—Week-days 7 A.M. to 7 P.M., Sunday 7 to 10 A.M., and 3 to 6 P.M., Letters by the English Mail are delivered in the Fort between 5 A.M. and 9 P.M., about forty minutes after the arrival of the steamer. Proceeding further north along Mayo Road the stranger will next pass the TELEGRAPH OFFICES : The main building for the Government and Eastern Telegraph Departments was completed at a cost of Rs. 2,44,697 on the 20th April, 1874. The south wing was afterwards added to the original building and opened in September, 1888, having cost Rs. 1,53,172. The Meteorological Office is in this building, the Telegraph

SECRETARIAT.

UNIVERSITY HALL.

Receiving Offices being on the ground floor, and fitted up with all conveniences for the speedy despatch of either inland or sea cable messages.

The employes of the department have quarters provided for their use in a spacious building on Waudby Road.

QUEEN VICTORIA's STATUE occupies a commanding position at the north end of the Mayo Road where that thoroughfare joins the Esplanade Road. The statue, one of the finest in the city, cost, including the pedestal and ornamental railings, Rs. 1,82,443, of which sum H. H. Kunderao, Gaekwar of Baroda, contributed Rs. 1,65,000. The statue, which is by Nobel, is of pure white marble. The late Queen is represented in a sitting posture, the chair of state in which she is seated being placed on an octagonal platform some eight feet in height, the whole covered by a canopy reaching to a height of 42 feet. The statue measures 7 feet 2 inches in height, and is a masterpiece of the sculptor's art. The features are excellent, while the delicate manner in which the regal robes, the ornamentation of the state chair, and the decoration of the pedestal and canopy have been treated, place the statue in the first rank as a work of art. The royal coat of arms is placed in a conspicuous position in front of the pedestal, while over the crown at the back of the chair is the Star of India, the Rose of England, and the " Lotus of India, " the mottoes " *Dieu et Mon Droit* " and " *Heaven's Light our Guide* " being placed around the emblems on the statue, which was unveiled by Lord Northbrook in 1872.

Having completed his tour of Mayo Road and its objects of interest, the visitor will now enter the Espla-

nade Road.   It will be observed that the road in question
commences about half-a-mile to the north of the statue,
and that it is bounded by two open spaces, the one on
the west known as the MARINE LINES and that on the
east as the GENERAL PARADE GROUND OR MAIDAN.   Before proceeding southward there are one or two buildings
that should be noticed, the first of which is the red brick
structure half hidden by the trees, and situated at the
corner of the Waudby Road.

THE GYMKHANA :   The building alluded to is the
pavilion of the Bombay Gymkhana Club, the membership of which is confined to Europeans.   Towards the
cost of the club which was founded in 1875, Sir Cowasjee
Jehangir contributed Rs. 5,000. Officers in His Majesty's
Service are admitted without ballot.   Entrance fee Rs.
20 ; monthly subscription, Rs. 4 (paid quarterly in
advance).   Non-residents on being duly proposed and
seconded may become honorary members.   To the
north of the pavilion and in the grounds are several
well-kept tennis courts, the members of the Gymkhana
during the cold season carrying out a series of sporting
events comprising mounted and dismounted sports, polo,
football, hockey, cricket, and an athletic meeting which
is generally well attended.

Opposite the pavilion on Waudby Road is the town
mansion of the Tata family, next to which, at the junction of the latter road with the Esplanade Road is the
ALEXANDRA GIRLS' SCHOOL.   The institution was pro-
moted and founded by the late Mr. Manockjee Cursetjee,
who as far back as 1841, became so deeply imbued with
a sense of the great need and importance of female

education on Western lines, that he contemplated the establishment of a public school where Indian girls could receive a befitting education in the English language. His unrelaxing efforts and example gathered around him a small body of Parsee and Hindu friends, who had learnt to accept the principle so boldly advocated by him that the moral advancement of the Indian people was based on female education. With their support and encouragement, both moral and material, the Alexandra Native Girls English Institution took its rise on the 1st September, 1863. It was so named after the Princess Alexandra of Wales (now her Majesty the Queen Consort of England) in commemoration of her marriage in that year.

In rear of the latter institution will be noticed several private residences which give a good idea of the later style of domestic street architecture adapted by residents. At the corner of the Napier Road are the offices of the BOMBAY CITY IMPROVEMENT TRUST and further down the same road, on the right will be found the FRERE FLETCHER SCHOOL, which owes its origin to the late Miss Prescott, who was instrumental in raising subcriptions for its erection and obtained a grant of land from Government. The school receives children irrespective of their creed or caste. The building, which is in the Italian Gothic style. measuring about 100 feet by 66 feet, consists of three floors.

Returning to the Esplanade Road and proceeding south the JOHN CONNON SCHOOL, is the next building to be noticed. It was erected at the joint expense of Government and the School Trustees, and is open for the education of boys and girls, the building, which is in the modern Gothic style, being well arranged internally. The Scottish Education Society, who control the management of the institution. have another school at Byculla, at the corner of Love Lane.

THE CHARTERED BANK BUILDINGS adjoin the Scotch High School. They are Classic-Renaissance in design, the frontage being an imposing one. At the apex of the pediment there is a fine group of figurative sculpture, representing Great Britain, India, Australia and China. This central feature is flanked by wings of imposing design, each having a small tower capped by domes. On the ground floor is situated the large hall, where the Bank business is transacted. The hall is 137 ft. in length by 77ft. in width and 28ft. high, the walls above being supported by handsome columns and arches. On the north side of the hall are the agent's and accountants offices, with brokers' waiting-room attached to the former. On the south side of the vestibule there is a general waiting-room.

At the junction of the Esplanade and Hornby Roads, are the offices of the Oriental Government Life Assurance Company, which occupy premises which, previous to enlargement, were up to 1896 used as the Cathedral High School for Boys.

The FLORAL FOUNTAIN which at this point is situated in the centre of the roadway was orginally intended to be erected in the Victoria Gardens at Byculla, but for various reasons the present site was afterwards selected. The fountain, which is enclosed within an iron railing, is of stone and surmounted by the figure of Plenty, other

CHARTERED BANK, ESPLANADE ROAD.

figures being placed at the angles of the several basins. The first object that is likely to attract the attention of the sight-seer after passing the above point is the fine range of buildings on the right hand side of the road, at the north of which are the attractive Fort premises of Messrs. Treacher & Co., General Merchants. In the line of buildings alluded to, which are all three storeys high and have a stone frontage with a continuous arcade below, will be found the BOMBAY CLUB one of the leading Clubs of the city. This range also contains several good shops, the upper floors being used as offices, while at the southern end will be seen the handsome stone building rendered conspicuous by its imposing frontage, the roof being supported on massive columns, in which is located the Bombay offices of the NATIONAL BANK. On the opposite side of the roadway at the corner of Medows Street is a fine block of buildings occupied by Commercial firms and a few doors further down the PAPER CURRENCY OFFICE, over which a Military guard is posted. It is of somewhat heavy design and consists of four floors. Over the counters the greater part of the paper currency of the Presidency is passed, the interior of the offices being fitted up with spacious bullion and note stamping rooms. Passing the University Gardens on the right and the premises of Messrs. Hoar & Co., and Thomas Cook & Son on the left, at the corner of Fuller Road will be found the ESPLANADE HOTEL, erected in 1869 of brick and iron. The entrance hall is embellished with a fine painted domed roof. The billiard-room is on the ground floor, the extensive dining-room being on the floor above.

Adjoining the hotel will be found the premises (destroyed by fire in 1896) of the Army & Navy Stores, the stone *facade* of which is designed with much taste, and set off with marble and granite columns.

The next building is the DAVID SASSOON MECHANICS' INSTITUTE, which has a   arfed appearance, alongside the other str   irround it. The institute, which cost £   ly the gift of the late Mr. David Sasso   tue stands in the entrance hall, and of   Albert Sassoon. Above the shops on the   here is a spacious Reading Room and Lib   64 feet by 30 feet in which at stated pe   s are given. In addition to thousands of   ther kinds of light reading, the scientific se   rary contains the largest and best collection of works on applied science in Western India. Visitors to Bombay are allowed to use the library on payment of Rs. 2 per month, or 8 annas per week, the quarterly subscription for residents being Rs. 6.

On the opposite side of Hope Street is the massive Cawasjee Jehangir building in which are located the ELPHINSTONE COLLEGE and GOVERNMENT RECORD OFFICE but which was originally designed to accommodate the Government Central Printing Press. It was subsequently enlarged and is now appropriated to the use of the Elphinstone College; and the storing of Official Records. The College previous to 1856 had been amalgamated with the Elphinstone High School, but in the latter year a separation took place, the institution being then located in the building facing the Victoria Gardens at

Byculla, now known as the Technical Institute. The late Sir Cawasjee Jehangir Readymoney contributed two lakhs of rupees towards the building which cost Rs. 7,41,497. A carved medallion of the donor is placed over the man entrance.

THE KING'S STATUE : This fine equestrian statue, which cost £12,500, stands in a prominent ·position on the roadway near the corner of Rampart Row. It was designed by Boehm and presented to the city by the late Sir Albert Sassoon to commemorate the visit of the King (then Prince of Wales) to India in 1875-6, and was unveiled in 1879. His Majesty who is dressed in a Field-Marshal's uniform, is represented as seated on horseback and holding his helmet in his right hand. The statue, which is 12 feet 9 ins. in height, stands on a massive granite base on the sides of which are two well executed bronze castings—one representing the landing at the Bombay Dockyard and the introduction of native Chiefs, and the other the presentation made by the children at the *fete* held on the Esplanade. The ends of the base are embellished with the royal coat-of-arms and the motto "*Ich Dien*" and a shield with a suitable inscription.

In Rampart Row are the P. & O. Company's Offices and those of Messrs. Sassoon & Co.'s both of which have attractive frontages. In the P. & O. Co.'s Offices the lower floor is alloted to the Freight Department, the Passenger Department, Waiting and Reading Room and Superintendent Offices being on the first floor. On the open space of ground in front of these offices it is proposed to erect the new Cathedral.

In the course of the previous portion of his tour, the visitor has been following a route laying outside the old walls of the city, but will now be conducted through what may be practically described as the heart of the district which is still locally known as the Fort. The fort was, from 1718 until the year 1863 when its demolition was commenced, enclosed within the ramparts that followed the course of Rampart Row, Esplanade Road, Hornby Road, and Fort Street, having gates at Apollo, Church Gate, and Bazaar Gate Streets. Less than sixty years ago, the Fort was not only the principal commercial centre of the town, but also included within its walls a considerable proportion of its inhabitants. Although the ramparts which surrounded the fort have been razed, most of the streets and lanes are much the same as they were in the olden times. The fort, which was dismantled, had walls about forty feet high and from twenty-five to fifty wide at the top. These carried guns, and were surrounded by trenches which were full of water during the rains. People used to take their evening walks on the rampart walls, and on the outbreak of fire in any part of the town a drummer traversed the wall from end to end, sounding the alarm.

Passing over the site of what was called the Apollo Gate, and entering the precincts of the Fort, the visitor will first find on the left hand at the corner of Apollo Street the ST. ANDREW'S CHURCH, or as it is sometimes called the Scotch Kirk, which was built in 1818 at a cost of Rs. 50,000. It contains a fine organ by Bishop and Starr, and has a gallery running round three of its sides. In 1827 the present steeple was erected, the old

GOVERNMENT DOCKYARD.—ENTRANCE GATES.

one having been destroyed by lightning in the year previous.

Adjoining the church is the round building known as the ICE HOUSE, which, in the days previous to the establishment of ice factories, was used for the storage of American block ice. The GREAT WESTERN HOTEL, which is well managed, was in former days the old High Court, and contains several extensive rooms.

Facing the hotel is the main entrance gate, surmounted by a clock tower, of the GOVERNMENT DOCKYARD, which covers an area of about 500,000 square yards, and was first opened in 1735, when the East India Company began building ships in Bombay. It has since that date been much enlarged and enclosed, many men-of-war having been erected on the slips since 1800, when the *Cornwallis*, a 74 gun frigate of 1,363 tons, was launched, the last vessel of this description built being the *Meanee*, of 4 guns and 2,400 tons, finished in 1847. A number of small crafts are still erected in the yard, but the principal portion of the work done now consists of repairs to the vessels of the Royal Navy and Royal Indian Marine on the station. A well equipped steam factory in the yard is capable of turning out all kinds of machine work for the above purposes, the recently lengthened and deepened Bombay and Duncan Dry Docks, originally constructed in 1736 and 1810, affording accommodation for the examination of the hulls of the largest men of war. The upper portion of the Duncan Dock has been converted into a torpedo boat dock. The Wet Dock, situated between the steam factory and Custom House, covers an area

o

of about five acres and is chiefly intended as a harbour for the naval vessels in the monsoon season. The dock can accommodate some twenty vessels of large tonnage, the wharfage being about sixteen hundred feet in length. At its south-west corner a Dry Dock is constructed to hold three torpedo-boats with a boat slip adjoining. In the building of the West Dock 1,100,000 cubic feet of masonry were used. The Dockyard is fitted with a complete electric light instalation.

A few doors past the hotel are the rooms and museum of the BOMBAY NATURAL HISTORY SOCIETY, which are well worth visiting, the collection of birds, fishes, and animals, though small, being arranged with much taste. The museum is located over the business premises of Messrs. Phipson & Co. Following the tram lines on the right will next be seen the OPIUM GODOWNS and the GOVERNMENT CENTRAL PRESS, the latter building, in which all the Government printing is done, being easily distinguished by its short chimney. Adjoining the Press is the CUSTOM HOUSE, which, with its unpretentious frontage, consists of a series of old buildings. Previous to the British occupation they were used as a Portuguese barracks.

In Bank Street will be found the fine premises occupied by the BANK OF BOMBAY and the BANK OF BENGAL, the former having an extensive frontage on Green Street, and the latter overlooking Elphinstone Circle.

Emerging out of Bank Street the visitor will enter Elphinstone Circle, which was built on what was formerly called Bombay Green. The Garden was completed about the time of the visit of the Duke of

Edinburgh, in 1872, the spacious blocks of building surrounding the Circle containing many of the offices of the leading mercantile firms. In the centre of the Garden, which is well laid out, is a large fountain, to the east of which will be found two statues, one of the Marquis Cornwallis and the other of the Marquis Wellesley.

Leaving the Garden by the north gate, the next building of note is the ST. THOMAS' CATHEDRAL. The authentic history of the Cathedral begins with the arrival in Bombay, on St. Matthew's Day, September 21st, 1714, of that excellent and earnest, if somewhat too impulsive and headstrong chaplain, the Rev. R. Cobbe. Although unprovided with a church until the end of the year 1718, the Government appears from the first to have been fully sensible of the claims of religion to some due observance. Chaplain or no chaplain, services were conducted, on Sundays, in a room within the castle walls. There are two silver chalices preserved in the muniment chest in the Cathedral, one bearing the date of 1632, with an inscription stating that it was " the gift of the Greenland Merchants of the cittie of York, " the other presented in 1675 by Gerald Aungier. About the year 1684 the Directors appeared to have first entertained the idea of the need of a church. The suggestion was warmly taken by the authorities in Bombay. A plan of a church was submitted for the Court's approval, the proposed edifice to be large enough to hold a thousand people, in order that there might be sufficient accommodation for natives if any cared to attend the services. The Company engaged to supply the

necessary balance, after subscriptions had been obtained
from local residents. The three chaplains of Bombay
and Surat were entrusted with the funds collected,
and were instructed to purchase materials, so that
there might be as little delay as possible in carrying out
the project, after receipt of authority from the Board of
Directors in England. A   selected in the Fort
that the church migl   a wu   is to the natives, and
for security. A su   fifty   iousand rupees was
collected, the build   ʻ   :ed, and the walls
actually carried to t   fifteen feet. Those,
however, were days of   ours of wars, and the
little English garrison   iuch as it could do to
hold its own against   ns of enemies who
constantly swooped down upon it. The building of the
new church was, no doubt, suspended during one of these
periods of storm. But when men began again to think
of completing the building, it was found that the funds
collected for this purpose had mysteriously disappeared.

The Honourable William Anislabile, Esq., General
and Governor of Bombay, etc., gave leave for the building of Bombay church June 19, 1715, and the first stone
was laid by Worshipful Stephen Strutt, Deputy Governor, November 18, 1715. The heavy and disagreeable
part of collecting subscriptions and the actual building of
the church occupied the next two and a half years. Far
and wide, throughout the whole of India then under
British rule, and even to China, went letters from the
energetic Cobbe, asking for help towards carrying out
his laudable scheme ; to Surat, Carwar, Madras, Calcutta,
Calicut, Anjengo, and Persia—not a single place where

GOVERNMENT DOCKYARD.—TORPEDO DOCK.

the Company's merchants were located was left un-
attacked and on the whole it must be confessed that
the requests for donations were met in a most liberal
spirit. The merchants of Surat must be counted among
the most liberal benefactors.

In addition to these applications for assistance sent to
various parts of India, a letter was written to the Honourable Court of Directors, in which, after thanking the
Directors for many favours such as "fresh provisions
and a passage gratis, and thirty pounds advanced in
England," Mr. Cobbe sent "the first fruits of my labours,
a list of all christenings, weddings, and burials which
have happened here since my arrival, and a catalogue
of the books contained in the Honourable Company's
Library." He then turns to the subject ever upper-
most in his thoughts, and, after thanking the Company
for their generous donation, says: "We hope your
Honours will be pleased to send us such useful and
necessary ornaments for our church, as cannot easily be
procured in these parts, such as a good ring of bells,
one large marble font, two branch or brass candlesticks,
and two tables in brass with the Creed, Lord's Prayer,
and Ten Commandments engraved thereon, with two
other tables in brass, whereon to inscribe the names of
our honourable and worthy benefactors."

At length the church was finished, and was opened on
Christmas Day, 1718. On Christmas Eve, Mr. Cobbe, the
chaplain, received the following letter from Mr. Owen
Phillipps, Secretary to Government:—"The church being
now finished so as divine service may be decently performed therein, the President has thought fit to order

me to inform you, it is his pleasure, to-morrow morning being, the nativity of our blessed LORD, you repair thither at the hour of ten, and perform the office according to the Liturgy of the Church of England as usual ; and to continue the service of the church as appointed on every day of the week at the hours of eight in the morning, and four in the aftern ... you are able to go through with it) exc ... lays, when the service is not to begin till te ... the church itself, it is indeed a structure d ... ired for its strength and beauty, neatness ... y, but more especially for its echo ; the ... g arched with three regular arches of st ... d by two rows of pillars and pillasters ... e with a large semi- dome at the east end to receive the communion table, like that of St. Paul's London, ascending by three steps, and a rail to separate it from the body of the church. Its situation is very commodious, in the midst of the inhabitants within the town wall, and at a due distance from the Fort. As to its extent, it is larger than either of the English churches at Madras or Bengal, or any of the Portuguese churches here ; suitable, in some measure, to the dignity of our Royal Settlement, and big enough for a cathedral. Thus was the ceremony of opening Bombay church performed with all public de- monstrations of joy, with that decency and good order, as was suitable to the solemnity." The church being eventually opened on Christmas Day, 1718, an enter- tainment being given by the Governor to the whole town in honour of the event, and salute fired from the Fort. In 1838 the present tower was added to the edifice at a cost of Rs. 16,000, the outlay on the clock being defrayed by public subscription. Since 1865 various additions have been made, the principal being the new chancel and organ chamber, the latter containing the organ built by Messrs. Bishop and Starr. In the interior of the Cathedral there is a fine monument of the Right Rev. Thomas Carr, the first Bishop of Bombay, who died in 1859, and a large number of handsome monuments and tablets, the inscriptions on which will well repay the trouble of perusal.

The most prominent memorials are in memory of the following persons :—

CHARLES JAMES MANSON, of the Bombay Civil Service, assassinated at Sooribund on the 29th May, 1858, while trying to suppress an intended insurrection of Mahratta Chiefs.

JONATHAN DUNCAN, Governor of Bombay from 1795 to 1811. Infanticide was abolished in Benares and Kathiawad doing his tenure of office.

MAJOR ELDRED POTTINGER, of the Bombay Artillery, whose successful defence of Herat, his gallant bearing and judicious counsel throughout the eventful period of the British reverses in Afghanistan, are recorded in the annals of his country. Compelled by long continued exertion, anxiety, and fatigue in the discharge of his public duty, to seek a change of climate for the recovery of his health; Major Pottinger was returning to England, *via* China, when he was attacked by malignant fever at Hong-Kong, where he died on the 15th of November 1843, aged 32 years.

LIEUT.-COL. JOHN CAMPBELL, who defended Mangalore during a siege of eight months against the united armies of Mysore and France.

LIEUT. CHARLES WALKER, who, with many others, was drowned when the transport *Castlereach* was wrecked on entering the harbour on 18th June, 1840.

" ENTERPRISE " MEMORIAL, erected in memory of 74 officers and crew of the Indian Marine Steamer *Enterprise*, which was lost in a cyclone at Port Blair, on the 2nd November, 1891.

DANIEL SETON, Governor of Surat Castle, who died in 1803.

LIEUT.-COL. ROBERT COY, fatally wounded by a rocket on the 4th January, 1779, while taking part in the expedition to Poona.

BRIGADE-MAJOR W. C. HARRISON, who was saved by three sepoys at the battle of Maiwand, and afterwards recovered from typhoid fever at Kandahar, but who when engaged in re-organising his regiment (Jacob's Rifles), was again attacked with fever and died at Venice on 12th January, 1882.

JOHN WATSON, Superintendent of the Presidency Marine and Commander-in-Chief of the Naval Forces, employed in the reduction of Salsette in 1774.

CAPTAIN E. M. ENNIS, of the 21st N. I., who was barbarously put to death between Sukkur and Hyderabad on the 18th February, 1843.

CAPTAIN GEORGE NICHOLAS HARDINGE, R.N., who commanded the *San Furenzo* of 36 guns and 186 men and chased and brought into action, upon three succes-

GOVERNMENT DOCKYARD.—DUNCAN DOCK.

sive days, the French frigate *La Piedmontaise* which vessel carried 50 guns and 566 men, bore a high character, and was the terror of the Indian Seas. Nobly supported by his officers and crew, he achieved a most brilliant conquest, but fell with glory on the last and critical period of this heroic enterprise, upon the 18th of March, 1808, and in the 28th year of his age. His ardent perseverance and skill in these actions were so extraordinary, that by unanimous votes, the House of Commons raised a monument in St. Paul's Cathedral, to his memory.

" CLEOPATRA " MEMORIAL, erected in memory of Commander Young and 150 officers and crew of the East India Company's steam frigate *Cleopatra*, which foundered off the Malabar Coast in April, 1847.

In addition to the above, the memorials to the following personages deserve mention :— Samuel John Croft Falconer ; Alexander Cunine Peal ; Thomas Mostyn ; Admiral Maitland ; Lieut.-Col. John Nugent ; Captain George Warden ; Major-General John Bellasis ; Lieut.- Col. C. B. Burr ; Captain F. McGillivray ; and John Fraser Heddle.

Services are held on Sunday, at 7-30 A.M. and 6 P.M.

The Cathedral stands at the entrance to Church Gate Street which half a century ago was not the busy and crowded thoroughfare of to-day. Yet it was regarded as a fashionable road, with the substantial houses of wealthy Parsees on either side. So far as the width of the street is concerned, it is just as broad as it was in the old days, and many of the houses there are also in much the same state.

Opposite the Cathedral will be noticed the Hong-Kong and Shanghai Bank, and the buildings in which are located the offices of the Royal Insurance Company and the Fort premises of Messrs. Kemp & Co., Chemists and Druggists. Passing the latter shop, in Parsee Bazaar Street, will be found the rooms of the CHAMBER OF COMMERCE. The o   ies of the Chamber are to encourage a frie   d unanimity among commercial men on all   lving their common good ; to promote and   general mercantile interests of the Preside   ct and classify information on all matte   commercial interest ; to obtain the removal,   an, of all acknowledged grievances aff   ants as a body, or mercantile interests in general ; to receive and decide references on matters of usage and custom in dispute, recording such decision for future guidance, and by such and other means assisting to form a code of practice for simplifying and facilitating business ; to communicate with the public authorities, with similar Associations in other places, and with individuals on all subjects of general mercantile interests ; and to arbitrate between parties to refer to, and abide by, the judgment of the Chamber.

Proceeding round the left side of the Circle gardens on the east will be observed the TOWN HALL. The suggestion to build a Town Hall was first made about eighty years ago, the work on the present building being commenced in 1821, and completed some twelve years afterwards at a cost of about five lakhs of rupees, partly received from the proceeds of lotteries and funds granted by the Directors of the East India Company. The building consists of a basement (in which is situated the office of the Surgeon-General, the District Staff Office, where Military Officers report their arrival and departure from Bombay), and an upper storey, and is about 260 feet long by 100 feet wide. The large hall contains a fine organ, costing about £3,000, given by Sir Albert Sassoon to commemorate the visit of the Duke of Edinburgh in 1872. The hall, which is frequently used for public meetings, concerts, and balls, also contains a statue of Mountstuart Elphinstone, Governor of Bombay from 1819 to 1827. A statue of Sir Charles Forbes is placed in the south vestibule and in the north vestibule are the statues of the following persons—Mr. Stephen Babington, Sir J. Malcolm, Mr. C. Norris, Lord Elphinstone, Sir Jamsetjee Jeejeebhoy, Sir Bartle Frere, and the Hon. Jugonath Sunkersett. The library and museums of the Bombay Branch of the Royal Asiatic, Society is located at the north end of the central hall, the Durbar Room, so called on account of its being used for State purposes previous to the completion of the Secretariat, being situated at the south-east corner of the hall, on the west side of which there is a handsome portico approached by a massive flight of stone steps from the Elphinstone Circle Gardens.

The CASTLE AND ARSENAL are immediately in rear of the hall. Bombay Castle is now all that remains to remind the visitor of the old fortifications. The building is well worth a visit, though permission to enter has to be obtained from the Military authorities. Inside the walls, which enclose an area of over 300 feet on either side, is a look-out tower with a clock and time-ball. The latter falls at 1 P.M. The Arsenal adjoins the Castle, and is the centre of supply of munitions of war to the Army of the Bombay Presidency.

On the right of Mint Road are the old TOWN BARRACKS, in which are located the Presidency Pay and Commissariat Offices, the Head-quarters of the Volunteer Artillery Corps, and the SHIPPING OFFICE, the latter being formerly the Officers' Messhouse. From an inscription on the wall of the barracks it would appear that they were built in 1803, and prior to the removal of the Military to Colaba were occupied by the East India Company's European Regiments.

Facing the barracks on the right of the Mint Road is the MINT, erected from designs of Major Hawkins, R.E., and opened about the year 1827, since which date it has been greatly enlarged. Before Government closed the Mint against private silver in June, 1893, the Bullion Room, must have been an interesting sight, filled with stores of silver in all its different forms. By law the Mint was compelled to accept and coin all silver handed in suitable for coinage and above a certain weight. The first step in the evolutionary stage of the rupee's career takes place in the Allegating Room, the metal being too soft to stand manipulation and the wear and tear of time. In this room copper is added to it to make the alloy, which becomes the rupee. The "allegated" boxes of silver and copper next pass to the Melting Room, where the metals are placed in large plumbago crucibles each of which contains nearly 1,600 tolas, and melted in

GOVERNMENT DOCKYARD.—THE BASIN.

in great iron furnaces. This melting room is an interesting sight, with its glowing furnaces, its powerful machinery, its crowd of bronzed figures running hither and thither, all busily engaged in the fierce heat, in their arduous task of transforming the white bars of glistening silver and bags of copper, into streams of transparent molten metal. When the melting is complete, the crucible is lifted out by a chain, champ, and pulley, and swung through the air to a line of rail, on which run the oiled moulds. These moulds are of iron and one side opens out. The crucible is then tilted over by machinery, and its contents poured into the moulds. The bars on being removed from the mould are placed to cool in a large tank of water, which hisses like a witch's cauldron when it receives its gleaming treasure. The ends of the bars, which are generally irregular, are then cut off by a powerful machine. The bars are then stored until the following day, when the assay report states whether they are correct or not. After being pronounced correct, the bars are removed to the Rolling Room where after passing through the rolling presses, they are taken to the Punching Room. This room contains rows of automatic machines which punch blank discs the size of a rupee out of the rolled straps with marvellous rapidity. The blank discs are taken to the Weighing Room, which is one of the most interesting rooms in the Mint. The Napier weighing machines used here are of the most delicate and perfect make, each of the 68 machines costs £300 and can weigh 23 rupees per minute, thus making a total of Rs. 5,00,000 in a day of six hours. The correct discs are taken

next to another machine, which gives each its raised
edges. After this process the blanks are subsequently
removed to the Stamping Room. Here the blank disc
receives its impression, which is done by two dies in a
powerful automatic machine, which turns out 80 to 90
rupees per minute. After stamping, the coins are removed to the Ringing F   very rupee is next
" rung," and all with a   picked out. The
rupee is now a *fait accom*   lution is complete,
and he has arrived at ad   before he can issue
from the Mint, he is aga   d tested. In front
of the Mint, is a large   surrounded by an
iron railing.

The visitor should ne   right at the end
of the Mint compound, but before doing so it may be as
well to inspect the THE RUTTONSEY MOOLJEE FOUNTAIN,
at the junction of the Frere Road. It is oriental in
design, consisting of a lower basin and drinking trough
for animals, and was erected at the expense of Mr.
Ruttonsey Mooljee, a wealthy Bhatia merchant, in
memory of his only son, a lad of about fifteen years of
age. The dome of the fountain is crowned by a statue
of the deceased.

THE PORT TRUST ADMINISTRATIVE OFFICES, which are
at the end of Ballard Road, are built of blue basalt with
Coorla stone facings, and consist of two wings standing
at right angles to each other, surmounted with a massive
look-out tower at the corner between the wings, one of
which faces the harbour. The building consists of four
storeys, inclusive of the ground floor, and is 72 feet high,
while the tower runs up 38 feet above the general build-

ing, which measures 148 feet on one wing, and 123 feet on the other, with a mean width of 60 and 50 feet, respectively, and a verandah 10 feet wide all around. On the ground floor are situated the Record-rooms of the various departments, the printing offices, and the engineer's plant and instrument rooms, with a strong-room and store-rooms for the Port Officer's and Light-house departments. The whole of the first floor is utilised by the Port Officer's department and general correspondence offices. A portion of the western or larger wing of the second floor is appropriated to the use of the board and chairman's room, the rest being occupied by private rooms for the secretary and his assistants, correspondence, cash, and book-keeping offices. On the top floor are located the engineering offices. At the main entrance, which abuts on to Ballard Road, there is a large hall leading to a fine circular staircase ascending to the top flat. The compound, which measures 300 by 125 feet, extends from Ballard Road on one side to Cochin Street on the other ; contains a coach-house and stable, and quarters for lascars, the remaining portion of the ground being neatly laid out as a garden. Over the main entrance there is a handsome facade with a beautiful *bas-relief* hewn in stone representing the Port Trust seal, supported on either side with nautical symbols. Running out into the harbour from the east of the above building, is the BALLARD PIER, where passengers by the outward mail steamers are landed, and their baggage examined by the Customs officials.

Proceeding northward along the harbour frontage the fine block of buildings in which are offices of the BRITISH

INDIA STEAM NAVIGATION COMPANY will be found on
the left. On the ground floor is the cash department,
the captains' waiting room, and the brokers' office. The
second floor is utilized as the claims, freight and portage
bills department and the third is for the Agent's office
and the passage department.

Thence turning to the left near the oil tanks and
crossing the Frere Road will be found the small entrance
gates leading to the ST. GEORGE'S HOSPITAL, to which
visitors are admitted to see patients between 5 p.m.
and 6 p.m. daily. The foundation-stone of the men's
hospital, which will be found at the far end of the drive,
was laid by H. E. Lord Reay on the 20th February,
1889. Though free from architectural ornamentation
the building presents a most imposing appearance, and
no better site could possibly have been selected for the
purpose. The history of the institution is not altogether devoid of interest. In the year 1859 or 1860, when
Government resolved to demolish the Fort defences and
removed the troops to the cantonment at Colaba, the
European General Hospital for the first time became a
purely civil institution. In 1861 the old building, which
was then occupied as a hospital in Hornby Row, was sold,
and the patients and the establishment moved into the
building that was formely occupied as an artillery
hospital in Fort George. But that site being afterwards
required for the present Victoria Terminus, they were
again turned out and put into the old artillery barracks,
which are still utilized as female wards. The Government, recognizing that it was necessary that better
provision should be made for the accommodation of the

ST. THOMAS' CATHEDRAL.

sick, several plans were submitted to them, but for one reason or another, none were approved until the end of 1863. In that year plans and estimates were sanctioned for a new hospital, and in May, 1864, the foundations of that hospital were actually put in, and had risen visibly above the surface when the operations of building suddenly ceased. It was then supposed that there was some difference of opinion between the Government of India and the local Government. The former did not approve of the plans of the building because they thought that it was not good enough for Bombay, and therefore the building operations came to a standstill, and those foundations, which cost nearly a lakh of rupees, now lie buried and forgotten under the ground in in front of the present Bombay Gymkhana. Eventually the present building was erected. The facade is of blue stone, which is considerably relieved by the terracotta projections above the windows, the building being erected on what are technically called arched basements, in accordance with the latest dictates of sanitary science, in order to keep off the damp, while all the floors are ventilated by earthenware pipe shafts passed through the walls.

The new hospital provides for a hundred beds. The building cost about Rs. 4,59,000 ; the cost of the entire hospital and out-buildings being nearly Rs. 9,00,000. There are in all three floors, the arrangements on each of which are most thorough in every way. The entrance is under a stately porch, and on arriving at the top of the entrance steps one finds himself in a spacious hall paved with Minton tiles, the

D

wards being placed on either side, with a grand staircas
in the centre of the hall giving access to the upper
floors. There are two wards on the north and south
sides of the building, each of which contains 14 beds,
and a third ward at the north end, containing 12 beds.
and a special ward to the south containing one bed.
There are two nurse   each wing. There
are besides very coi   ig and reading-rooms
for the use of pati   m the ground floor.
On the ground floo   of the building are
the dispensary, apc   m, overseer's office,
steward's and other   The staircase leading
to the first floor i   alustrade, which is
surmounted with a   wood and holding in
the paws the shield   having iron railings
of neat design. On   going to the north,
is a pretty little chapel for the use of the patients. Next
to the chapel is the physician's room, and on the same
floor are a dining-room, two nurses' rooms, and two
wards accommodating 14 patients each. There is a special
ward on the same floor which contains only one bed.
There are again the operating-room, which is lighted
by means of sky-lights, and the dark-room for ophthal-
mic examinations. On the second floor, which
commands an excellent view of the eastern harbour, are
the physician's office, a dining-room, a reading-room, a
nurse's room, and two special wards in each wing, in
addition to two wards containing 14 beds each. The top
floor has the advantage of the other floor in that it has
in addition to its fine corridors, an extensive terrace
commanding a grand view of the greater part of the

city.   A lift is provided for carrying the patients on to the first and second floors.

The hospital stands on an extensive plot of ground which through the liberality of Government has been tastefully laid out as a garden on the western side of which are the quarters of the Lady Superintendent and nurses and a detached bungalow which has been provided for the House Surgeon, the buildings having been constructed in a style quite in keeping with that of the new hospital.   In the hospital there are 38 free beds, while in the other wards the charges are as follows :— Nos. 3 and 4 wards, 28 beds, Re. 1; No. 2 ward, 14 beds, Rs. 2 ; and No. 1 ward, 14 beds, Rs. 3 per day ; while in addition there are five private rooms for which the charge is Rs. 10 per diem.

A new block of buildings for a women's hospital is being erected to the north at a cost of five lakhs of rupees. The style of architecture will harmonise with the men's wards, and the two sections will be joined by an arched corridor over the roadway, so that the hospital, when finished will present a most imposing appearance.   In connection with the hospital a Convalescent Home has been opened at Khandalla, 78 miles from Bombay, consisting of wards for either sex, the charges for beds in the wards being Rs. 2 and Rs. 3 per day, or for a private room Rs. 5.   Though primarily intended for patients from the St. George's Hospital, accommodation is generally available in the Home for convalescents from all parts of India.   Applications for admission should be made to the Physician in charge of the St. George's Hospital.

Retracing his steps to the gate by which he entered the hospital ground, the visitor will, on turning to his right, pass the Victoria Terminus of the Great Indian Peninsula Railway opposite which are the magnificent Municipal Offices, the lofty domes of both buildings towering high above the neighbouring structures.

THE VICTORIA TERMINUS and Administrative Offices of the G. I. P. Railway ιpany, form one of the most handsome and promin buildings in the city, the station being the fine nd in the country. It is in the Italian Gothic; ; a frontage on the Hornby Road of oι et. The passenger terminus was opened ι 1882, the Adminis-trative Offices being bι⊤ ⌁e some three years later. The station platforms are roomy and afford ample accommodation for passenger traffic. Under the lofty roofs are located the necessary waiting and refresh-ment-rooms and a handsome booking-hall, with tesse-lated pavement, the walls and roof being decorated in blue and gold, and the roof and entrance doorway supported on graceful marble pillars. This hall is well worth a visit, as is also the main staircase of the Administrative Office building. The latter building forms three sides of a square enclosing an ornamental garden, the entrance gates of which are surmounted by a massive lion and tiger carved in stone. The offices consist of a ground and two upper floors, the most prominent feature of the building being the high tower rising over the centre portion and which is surmounted by a large figure of " Progress." There is a fine statue of the Queen-Empress placed in front of the building

below the clock. Passengers proceeding from this station by train should drive up to the entrances on the Hornby Road side.

THE MUNICIPAL OFFICES were opened in 1893, the corner stone having been laid by Lord Ripon, a former Viceroy of India. The late Mr. F. W. Stevens, the architect of the Railway Terminus, has designed the offices in keeping with the handsome structures by which they are surrounded, and has based his ideas on the early Gothic style of architecture, treating it with an Oriental feeling, as exemplified by the many domes that are to be seen rising above the gabled roofs of the building. The imposing facade, with its massive and lofty tower, surmounted with a dome, is flanked by two wings of the building which abut on the Hornby and Cruickshank Roads. The building does not at first appear to be so large as it really is, but on a closer inspection, the dimensions of the respective wings, each of which consists of a ground and two upper floors, stand out in greater prominence, and the tower, which rises to a height of some two hundred and thirty-five feet from the ground, looks very imposing. The carving which has been so artistically placed around the outside of the new offices stands out most prominently, especially the figures of the winged Venetian lions over the entrance porches, and the arms of the Corporation, the reproduction of the latter placed over the main facade being in itself an undoubted work of art reflecting credit on the native artisans whose labours have done so much to beautify the exterior of the building. The site of the edifice may be described as resembling the letter V with the lower point cut off, thus forming the southern face of the building, over which rises the tower. The building is approached by main entrances on the south and west, while over the facade rises a colossal allegorical figure representing " *Urbs prima in Indis."* The main staircase, is a splendidly executed piece of work, winding up the tower and is   ith a dome richly panelled and decorate   of cream and gold. The tower is one of t]   ie city.

The floors in both ·   n divided into lofty and commodious offi   veral departments, the Commissioner's ar   y's offices being in the Western wing. Th   iber, which measures about 65 feet in lengt   breadth, and is 38 feet in height, is situat   t floor at the north-west extremity of the Cruickshank Road wing, and on it the artchitect has evidently bestowed much care. It is approached from the wide and handsome corridors hrough large and beautifully moulded doorways, whose a pitals are richly carved and filled in overhead with oloured glass. At the northern end of the room is a large ornamental bay window filled with stained glass, having introduced therein the arms of the Corporation, the window being flanked on either side by stone canopied recesses. Glancing around, the spectator cannot but be struck with the light and airy appearance of the hall, despite its massive and impressive interior, it being open on the western, northern and eastern sides, and being well ventilated, by means of openings in the upper stained glass windows that are placed at regular intervals in the walls. These windows are set in arches,

having handsome marble column supports, richly carved
and decorated, while the ceiling, which is of unpolished
teak, is panelled and richly moulded and picked out
with gilt lines after a somewhat oriental design, and is
supported on corbels the subjects of which are different
castes of natives of India, each bearing a shield, on
which is placed some device forming a portion of the
Municipal arms or monogram.

There are two overhead galleries for the general
public, approached by separate staircases. The form or
the Council Chamber has, it is understood, been designed
in accordance with well-known examples, in order to
ensure the best acoustic results, while the seats and table
for the accommodation of the members of the Corporation have been arranged in a manner to suit the requirements of the Councillors. The hall is illuminated by
electric light, which is suspended overhead in three
handsome wrought brass electroliers of exquisite design,
each containing thirteen lights of 1,500 candle-power,
or 4,500 candle-power in all.

Proceeding northward along the Hornby Road past
the Terminus and the Municipal Offices, the imposing
"TIMES OF INDIA" BUILDING will be next noticed, in
which is printed the leading local daily newspaper.
Flanking one side of the main entrance to the building
is a tablet bearing the following inscription: "1838—
1901. This Stone was laid in the First Year of the
Twentieth Century, being the Sixty-Third Year of
Publication of the "Times of India." The building is
designed in the Indo-Gothic style, and presents a striking
appearance, the road frontage being embellished with

various gables and domed towers. The editorial and manager's offices are on the first floor, while in the spacious printing hall in rear are carried on all the various details connected with the management of one of the best equipped and largest newspaper and publishing firms in the east.

Adjoining the above offices is the ANJUMAN-I-ISLAM SCHOOL. The Anjuman-i-Islam was founded about fifteen years ago by some of the leading members of the Mahomedan community for the purpose of bringing about some amelioration in the condition of their co-religionists of Western India. The Mahomedan community had long been convinced that, while under the benign influence of the British Government, the other communities were making moral, social, intellectual, and political progress, their co-religionists were lagging behind in the race of life. They therefore came to the conclusion that the main, if not the sole, cause of the backward state of the community was the absence of education upon the western system. An application was accordingly made to Government to help them in their efforts in the direction of promoting English education among the community, and the Government of Sir Richard Temple complied with their request by promising an annual grant of Rs. 6,000. The Municipal Corporation also sanctioned a grant of Rs. 5,000 per annum, and with the assistance of these funds, added to their own private subscription, and the fees collected from the pupils, they have worked their schools steadily up to the High School standard. The Mahomadan community raised altogether Rs. 1,10,000 for building the

VICTORIA TERMINUS.

school, besides Rs. 50,000 which was set apart as endowments for the institution. The Government granted a free site, and also promised to contribute Rs. 38,000 towards the construction of the school-house, the foundation-stone of which was laid by Lord Reay on the 31st March, 1890. The building is in the Sarascenic style, the modern requirements for the construction of a school, and the harmonising of it with the several public buildings surrounding it being borne in mind. The school has three turrets, surmounted with domes of Porebunder stone, two of them being erected at the southern, and one at the northern facade of the structure. The tower is 125 feet high, and is capped with a dome having a circumference of 16 feet. The facade of the building, as also the tympanums and drums of the domes, the lower frieze and the arched wings of the several windows, are ornamented with coloured tiles. The general facing is of dressed blue stone, the several columns and the arches being made of Porebunder and yellow Coorla stones, relieved in places by red Hemnugger stone. The capitals of the front columns bear carvings of various pretty designs. Over the windows are placed stones carved in various geometrical designs. On the ground floor are four large and two small class-rooms, there being also apparatus, library and masters' rooms. On the first floor there are four class-rooms and a large hall measuring 63 feet long and 37 feet wide, with a gallery above it. The second floor has four class-rooms, which are very lofty and airy. There is no lack of ventilation in the school, which has spacious verandahs on either side of it. The school was opened by Lord Harris, on the 27th day of February, 1893.

Adjoining the latter building is the INDO-BRITISH INSTITUTION. This school was founded in 1838 by the Rev. G. Candy, and has for its object the education of the poor children of Indo-Britons. Ordinarily the greater number of children are clothed, boarded, and educated *gratis*, but a few of the pupils pay the full fee of Rs. 16 per mensem. The foun   xisting school was laid by the Earl of Duffe   h the compound in front of the school is H(IURCH, a small but neatly designed structi   ipposite side of the road will be observed th   ers of the SALVA- TION ARMY and the sm   building known as the JAFFER SULEMAN DIS   ssing further along the left hand side of the   nger will do well to pay a visit to the Wor   ¡POTTERY WORKS, which are situated in well laid out grounds, and in which are to be seen specimens of pottery and other wares manufactured by local artisans. In the same grounds, but somewhat further north, will be seen the SCHOOL OF ART or to give it its full title, the Sir Jamsetjee Jeejeebhoy School of Art, which was opened in 1857. The building is 275 feet in length, and contains four general class-rooms. The students are instructed in engraving wood, decorative painting, architectural sculpture, ornamental sculpture, and kindred crafts. The Lord Reay Art Workshops are situated in the grounds of the above building, and are well worth a visit. Within the main building is a small collection of paintings, destined eventually, it is hoped, to form the nucleus of a Picture Gallery worthy of the city.

The POLICE HEAD-QUARTERS are to be found in the large and handsome building at the corner of the Hornby and Carnac Roads. It is in the domestic Gothic style of architecture and consists of a ground and two upper floors. The police premises, occupying as they do a commanding position, have been designed in a manner that makes them rank among the best in the city, the yellow Coorla stone, which has been largely used in construction, being relieved by the interpositions of wooden beams and cross stays, the upper portions of the structure being decidedly Elizabethan. The general outline is broken by various projections in the form of the building, the main gable roof being surmounted with a turret some forty feet in height. The sky line is also relieved by other suitable designed terminals of a staircase tower, the one at the east corner having an octagonal dome surmounting it. The Offices of the Commissioner and Deputy Commissioner of Police are on the first floor, the officer in charge of the Conveyance and the Criminal Investigation Department Offices being on the ground floor. The upper storey is divided into residential quarters for European police officers, while to the rear of the extensive grounds are separate quarters for 120 Native Police Sepoys, and stables and quarters for 20 Mounted Sowars.

At the opposite corner of the Hornby Road, and occupying the triangular piece of land between that thoroughfare and the Carnac and Pultan Roads, are the CRAWFORD MARKETS. The main building is set apart for the sale of fruit and vegetables, and consists of a central hall with three main entrances. It is sur-

mounted at the north-west corner by a clock-tower, two
of the openings over the main entrances being filled
with sculptured marble tablets. Inside the building,
which covers an area of 56,000 square feet, is a fountain
presented by the late Sir Cowasjee Jehangir. The time
to see the market at its best is in the early morning,
when during the seaso~ ·~~ ·~·~·~~t fruit from all parts
of the Presidency can '   The Pedder Meat
and Fish Markets are ;   :parate buildings to
the west and facing tl   ad, the intervening
space between them an   narket being taken
up by a small and well   at the south end of
which there are a num   ; the sale of poultry,
game, birds, and small   ets. The markets,
which were completed ;   Rs. 11,18,500, owe
their origin to Mr. Arthu   a late Commissioner
of Bombay.

   At this point the stranger will find himself in the
vicinity of one of the most crowded districts of the native
town. The range of shops on the north side of the
Carnac Road will be found occupied by native trades-
men, while in rear are situated the cloth bazaars in
Shaik Memon Street, where will also be found the
handsome JUMA MUSJID, the principal Mohammedan
place of worship in the City. Within the triangular
piece of ground bounded on the south by Carnac Road
and its other two sides by Abdul Rehman Street and
the Kalbadavie Road will be found a tide of seething
Asiatic humanity, which ebbs and flows through the
chief mercantile thoroughfares. Nowhere can be seen
a livelier play of hues, or gayer and busier city life.

MUNICIPAL OFFICES.

Besides the endless crowds of indigenous Hindoo, Guzerati, and Maharatta people—coming and going, some in bright dresses, but mostly next to none at all, between the rows of grotesquely-painted houses there are to be studied specimens of every nation of the East-Arabs from Muscat, Persians from the Gulf, Afghans from the Northern frontier, shaggy black Belooches, negroes of Zanzibar, islanders from the Maldives and Laccadives, Malagashes, Malays and Chinese throng and jostle with Parsees, Jews, Rajputs, Fakirs, Portuguese, Sepoys, and Sahebs.

Allowing that the stranger has paid a brief visit to the above locality and afterwards returned to the Carnac Road, he will, on proceeding westwards along the latter thoroughfare, find on his right the VOLUNTEER RIFLES HEADQUARTERS, formerly the old Shipping Office, and a little beyond the SMALL CAUSES COURTS, the latter being located in a range of very old and unsuitable buildings. On the opposite side of the thoroughfare will be seen a range of attractive edifices, the first approached after passing the compound of the Police Headquarters being the GOCULDASS TEJPAL HOSPITAL, completed in 1874. This hospital is set apart for the exclusive use of natives. It cost Rs. 3,67,465, towards which sum the late Mr. Rustomjee Jamsetji Jeejeebhoy and Mr. Goculdass Tejpal each contributed £15,000. The site for the building was given by Government. The institution, which has accommodation for about 150 patients, being supported by the Municipality. THE HARRIS MEMORIAL SCHOOL is the next building to be passed, after which will be noticed the ST. XAVIER'S COLLEGE which stands in the ad oining compound, and will be recognised by its octagon-shaped tower. The institution is under the control of the priest-hood, and is built in the shape of a hollow square, the large class-room on the first floor having a semi-religious appearance. The St. Xavier's School, a new building opened in 1891, is in rear of the above college on th   Road, and, though capitally designed for   to which it is put, it does not present a·   ctural appearance.

Facing the ornam   : that stands in the centre of the roadwa¡   ¡ a site at the junc-tion of the Kalba   aum Roads, is the MONEY SCHOOL, foun   ds of the late Mr. Robert Cotton Mone¡   ect of both aiding in the diffusion of   ¡dge in its higher branches among the p·   -   untry, and of com-bining with it sound religious instruction. To the west of the above school is a large tank, adjoining which is the FRAMJEE CUWASJEE INSTITUTE. On the upper floor is a large hall occasionally used for entertainments and public meetings, and containing several portraits of well-known philanthropic natives. On the ground floor are the rooms of the Native General Library.

The low range of buildings facing the hall comprise the regimental lines of one of the regiments of Bombay Native Infantry, the Parade Ground being to the south.

Leaving the Dhobie Talao locality on the right, and turning to the left, the visitor, if he follows the tram route along the Cruickshank Road, on entering that thoroughfare, find himself in front of the ELPHIN-STONE HIGH SCHOOL. The building is easily recognised by the massive flight of stone steps leading to the main entrance gates. The School was founded originally in 1822 under the name of the Native Education Society's School. Sir Albert Sassoon contributed one-and-a-half lakhs of rupees towards the erection of the building, which is 452 feet in length. It contains nearly thirty class-rooms; the spacious central hall on the first floor measuring 65 by 35 feet, and is surrounded by a gallery. A covered-in play-ground runs under the central portion of the school.

In rear of the School is the Dinshaw Petit Gymnasium. The pavilion and grounds of which are well provided with all the necessary appliances for developing the physique of the pupils. Passing the St. Xavier's School, already briefly alluded to on page 65, the next building of interest will be found to be the CAMA HOSPITAL, which excellently managed institution was opened on 30th July, 1886, and bears the name of Mr. Pestonjee Hormusjee Cama, a wealthy Parsee inhabitant, who contributed Rs. 1,64,311 towards its erection. It contains 60 beds, and is intended for the sole use of women and young children of all castes and denominations.

In the same compound will be found a smaller building known as the ALLBLESS OBSTETRIC HOSPITAL, adjoining which are the ESPLANADE POLICE COURTS. The Courts were erected from the designs of Mr. John Adams. The work was commenced on the 3rd December, 1884, and completed on the 31st December, 1888, the building, which cost Rs. 3,73,694, being opened for business in May, 1889. It has a frontage of about 300 feet, and is erected in the medieval Gothic style, the roof, which is 100 feet from the ground level, being surmounted by a spiral shaft 45 feet in height. Entering the building under the carriage porch, on the ground floor will be found the Police Club Rooms, the Police Office, and the range of cells set apart for prisoners. On the first floor are the private rooms and court of the Third Presidency Magistrate, the Advocates' Library, and Clerks' room, and on the second floor the rooms and Court of the First Presidency Magistrate (who is also the President of the Marine Court of Bombay), together with the offices of the chief and other judicial clerks. The two courts are both light and lofty apartments, measuring 66 feet by 50 feet, and, in addition to being well furnished, have handsome teak roofs. Spacious verandahs run round the building, while at the south end of the structure is a separate staircase (filled with stained glass windows), for use of the general public, giving access to both courts, which are open from 11 a.m., to 5 p.m., and are worth a visit from those desirous of studying the criminal life of the country.

Having again arrived at the open space in front of the Railway Terminus, the statue of Dr. T. Blaney will be seen standing in front of the triangular Hornby Road Garden. Leaving the Gaiety Theatre on his left and passing down the Waudby Road which skirts the maidan, the FREE CHURCH OF SCOTLAND will be noticed. The church provides accommodation for 250 people, and is a handsome building, in which Coorla and Porebunder stones have been used, together with artistically worked teakwood gables and weather shades for the entrances,

the main one of which is protected by a porch. The interior of the building is furnished throughout in teakwood; the seating accommodation being well arranged, and a handsome pulpit of the same material forming a conspicuous object at the south-east end of the building. A commodious vestry adjoins the church.

Passing the church and turning to the left on the right hand will be noticed the Novelty Theatre and on the left the MASONIC HALL; the foundation stone of which was laid by Lord Sandhurst on the 5th June, 1897. The main hall, 60 feet by 30 feet, and 27 feet high, is on the first floor; the banqueting hall below being of the same dimensions. Rooms are provided in the building for the holding of chapters, and a dining-hall in close proximity to the banqueting hall. The construction of the building and furniture cost nearly one-and-a-half lakhs. Adjoining the hall are the Elphinstone Cricket Club and Fort Dispensary buildings.

Turning into the Hornby Road and proceeding south, on the left will be observed the Jamsetjee Jeejeebhoy Institute, a lofty building of four floors, with an arcade extending over the footpath.

The zig-zag manner in which the old houses on this side of the thoroughfare are built, and appear in some cases to have been almost dovetailed into one another, is due to the fact that they followed the various lines of the city ramparts which they formerly overlooked. Since the latter were razed to the ground, and Hornby Road formed directly over the foundations, several of the older houses have either been rebuilt or had their frontages brought forward. The Fort Fire Brigade Station and

B

Alice Buildings having lately taken the place of some of the old residences, which in this locality are almost exclusively occupied by Parsees, the town residence of Sir Jamsetjee Jeejeebhoy, the Parsee Baronet, being located close to the J. J. Institution mentioned above, while in the line of buildings will be noticed two Fire Temples, one to the north ɛ   ) the south of Alice Buildings.

On the right ha   oadway a fine range of handsome build‹   tected in recent years, in which will be f‹   he offices of leading, banking commerc   ops occupied by the principal Europeaɪ   Among the buildings worthy of notice ɛ   ied by Messrs. King, King & Co., the ؟   Company of Canada, Messrs. Macmillan & Co., Raja Deen Dayal, Messrs. Whiteway, Laidlaw & Co., The Japan Bank, and Messrs. John Roberts & Co., the latter firm having their show rooms on the ground floor of the FORT READING ROOM AND LIBRARY, one of the most tastefully designed buildings on this thoroughfare.

A short distance down Outram Road, a thoroughfare on the right of Hornby Road will be found the building of the CATHEDRAL HIGH SCHOOL for boys, opened in 1896. It appears that the school for boys has been the outcome of more than one educational effort, its early history being closely connected with that of the Bombay Diocesan Education Society's High School in Love-Lane, Byculla, and the Cathedral Choir School in the Fort. These two Schools were amalgamated in 1878 under the name of the Cathedral High School. It was in March,

1878, that an application was made to Government for a site on the Esplanade for the proposed school buildings, which was granted at the junction of the Hornby and Esplanade Roads. The block of buildings now occupied by the Oriental Life Assurance Company was erected there from funds obtained from Government, the S. P. C. K., and various other sources, the amount of cost aggregating over two lakhs of rupees. Soon after the building had been occupied, it was found that it was unsuitable for a school in many ways, and a resolution was passed by the governing body in September, 1886, appointing a sub-committee to enquire whether there is any other site to which the school could be moved with advantage, and whether Government would consent to facilitate the transfer. The resolution was forwarded to Government in October, 1886, but the matter was not finally disposed of until May, 1889, when sanction was given to the transfer on certain conditions, and the original building having been sold, with the proceeds of the sale the present building was erected. The management of the school is vested in a governing body constituted as follows:—President—The Lord Bishop of the Diocese ; Vice President—The Ven'ble the Archdeacon of Bombay and Senior Presidency Chaplain ; the Garrison Chaplain ; the Chaplain of Byculla ; the Chaplain of Colaba ; three Lay Communicants of the Church of England, nominated by the Trustees of the Cathedral ; three Lay Communicants of the Church of England, nominated by the Diocesan Board, and additional members nominated by the governing body.

The extraordinary and rapid growth of the school
is proof, if proof were needed, that it has supplied
a very real educational need in Bombay. In 1875
the choir school opened with 26 pupils, whereas at
the present time the number is about 200. The
extreme length of the main building is 126' 9" and
breadth, including the   south side, is 111',
and consists of a groun   per floors. Its total
height is 53' 6". The g   affords accommodation for three class roc   by 21'; one school
room 65' by 24'; a sta   le 24' by 24'; boys'
refectory 30' by 24',   achers' rooms, dispensary, godown, and   servants. A corridor 8' in width runs   ilding in front and
rear of the main room   or contains a chapel
24' by 21' 6", three class   us each 24' 6" by 21' 3"; an
office and library with quarters for the headmaster. On
the second floor there are two dormitories, one 44' by
25' and the other 76' 6" by 25', affording accommodation
for 44 beds. There are also provided two bed-rooms for
masters and a room for the matron.

Almost facing the Schools will be seen the GYM-
KHANA RACQUET COURT, which is located in a stone building with high walls. Opposite the school is the recently
opened LYING-IN HOSPITAL FOR PARSEES, easily recognised by its exterior being mainly constructed of blue
coloured bricks.

THE CATHEDRAL GIRLS' SCHOOL is located on Napier
Road, near Messrs. Whiteway and Laidlaw's establishment, in a substantial and well designed modern building, which externally presents many attractive features.
The visitor having now been again escorted to the
Floral Fountain, his tour round the Esplanade and Fort
may be appropriately brought to a conclusion.

CRAWFORD MARKET.

Colaba.

THE stranger wishing to visit Colaba and the southern portion of the island should again select the Wellington Fountain as his starting point, and having passed the Apollo Hotel, and proceeding along Colaba Causeway, he will see on his right the WESLEYAN METHODIST CHURCH, a well designed edifice with a lofty spire, the foundation stone of which was laid by Lord Reay.

On the same side of the road are the Tramway Company's Car Sheds and Offices. The Bombay Tramway Company has its head offices in New York, but the local depots are not only architecturally attractive, but are built on the most approved plans, and provide accommodation for a large number of horses for the double and single horse cars running on the Company's lines. Attached to the stables are extensive car erecting and repairing shops, there being other large car sheds and stables on the Parel and Falkland Roads. The Company, which practically commenced working in

1873, has now over twenty miles of track laid through the principal thoroughfares of the city and suburbs. The main line runs from the Sassoon Dock, Colaba, to Parel, while other branch lines run to Girgaum, Grant Road, Wari Bunder and Mazagon, which are intersected by other lines running across various parts of the city. It is contemplated to substitute electric for horse traction at a future date.

To the east of the red brick building facing the stables, used as the company's fodder store, is the SALUTING BATTERY. The stranger next passes the large open space known as the COTTON GREEN which, during the cotton season, is one of the busiest places in the city. The Green, so called, extends for about half-a-mile in length on both sides of the road and is used for stacking bales of pressed and unpressed cotton, the greater proportion of which is brought down from up-country to the adjacent Goods Stations of the G. I. P. and B. B. & C. I. Railways, and is here sold previous to shipment to Europe.

On the left hand side of the road, near Arthur Bunder, are erected the Cotton Exchanges, and facing the bunder itself the two large blocks of buildings known as "Grant's Buildings" which are now let out in tenements to Europeans. The COTTON EXCHANGES belong to the Bombay Cotton Trades Association and the Bombay Cotton Exchange Company. The former is in the early Gothic style of architecture. It consists of two lofty floors with a tower some fifty feet in height at the north-east corner. On the ground floor, facing the Causeway, is a large open hall 36 by 29 feet for the use of the general body of merchants and buyers and all connected with the trade, leading from which is a long apartment 60 by 40 feet, which is divided into six offices, for the use of firms engaged in the cotton business. There is a large Exchange room above, which measures some 90 by 40 feet, and which is provided with counters and racks for the exhibition and sale or purchase of cotton, while other facilities are also offered to the members of the Association for the transaction of business. The other Exchange consists of lower and upper floor, with a tower at the south-west corner, and has been erected principally of stone and blue brick. On the lower floor are the Exchange room and eight separate rooms for firms, while on the floor above is the cotton sale-room. The latter Exchange was principally built by natives interested in the cotton trade.

To the south of Arthur Bunder are to be seen the tall chimneys and high buildings of several of the local Cotton Mills and Presses.

Still continuing his journey southward the visitor will next pass the GUN CARRIAGE FACTORY, where large numbers of native artisans are employed under European supervision, the several shops in the yard being provided with a variety of machines for building all classes of gun transport and other military carriages and wagons. The Factory is connected by a siding with the B. B. & C. I. Railway, the latter Company having a basin and jetty at this point for the landing of stores received from Europe. Proceeding past the range of cotton godowns on the left of the road will be seen the Clock Tower over the entrance gates to the SASSOON

Dock. The Dock was excavated out of the solid rock by Messrs. Sassoon & Co., and was the first of the wet docks to be built in Bombay. In the trooping season the reliefs and drafts for the British Army in India are landed at the dock, where there is a spacious troop shed with officers' and women's quarters. The dock being in direct railway com   means of a branch line, the troops are   ical trains from the wharf up-country, th   being at Deolali on the G. I. P. Railway,   les from Bombay.

About half-a-mile t   e road the OFFICERS' SANATARIUM will be   left and the COLABA DEPÒT on the right.   ing the cold season provides temporary   h for the drafts and details of up-country   ring or departing by the troopships. Alth   anent buildings are few in number, during the trooping season lines of tents are pitched for the accommodation of the troops on the vacant space between the roadway and the buildings.

A short distance further along the road will be found the OFFICERS' MESS bungalow of the British Infantry Regiment, opposite which and placed low down on the foreshore is the SOLDIERS' SWIMMING BATH, constructed in such a manner that the water in the bath is changed at each tide.

The stranger will then notice rising before him the lofty spire of ST. JOHN'S CHURCH. The church, the lower tower and spire of which is 198 feet high, was built in memory of the officers, non-commissioned officers, and private soldiers who fell by sickness or in battle in the campaigns of Sind and Afghanistan during the years

ESPLANADE POLICE COURTS.

GENERAL POST OFFICE.

1838-43. The names of the officers are inscribed on tablets in the chancel. Special memorials to the officers who died during the late Afghan War were also erected in 1882. The altar wall has been decorated with tile mosaic by the 19th Regt. N. I., in memory of three of their officers; a reredos has been erected by the friends of twelve officers of various corps; the altar has been given in memory of two officers; and a rich marble pavement in memory of those who were Brethren of the Guild of the Holy Standard. The General Memorial of all the officers, non-commissioned officers, and men of the Bombay Army was erected over the principal entrance during 1883. The colours of the old 24th N. I. are preserved in the building.

Continuing his journey along the roadway leading past the church, the visitor will then find himself within the area set apart for the barracks of the European troops in garrison, which comprise three companies of artillery and a regiment of infantry. The artillery are quartered to the left and the infantry to the right of the main road. The barracks are some of the best to be found in the country, and are spacious and well ventilated. The STATION HOSPITAL is to the left of the road and nearly opposite the Parade Ground, on the Back Bay side of which are the rifle ranges. At the south-west corner of the Parade Ground is the Artillery Officer's Mess, and at the south-east corner a small Roman Catholic Chapel for the troops. In the grounds opposite the Chapel is a well furnished gymnasium, for the use of the troops.

A few yards further on is the entrance to the OBSER-

VATORY GROUNDS, containing buildings in which the various meteorological and other observations are recorded. At the summit of the slight rise in the roadway beyond this point will be seen the OLD COLABA LIGHTHOUSE, the light of which was discontinued in 1874 on the completion of the Prongs Lighthouse. The lantern has since been removed, the tower being now used as a military look-out station. At the foot anc   f the Colaba Road, will be noticed on the   ty leading to the shore and to the Colab: uth Forts ; adjoin-, ing which is the entran   COLABA CEMETERY, which has long since ce: or interments. The cemetery contains a n   monuments, principally erected to the   p captains, men of the Royal and East In   to the soldiers of the British and East   's European Regiments. Behind the hi   vest of the graveyard is the old Lunatic Asylum.

A little over a mile distant S. W. by S. from Colaba Point is the PRONGS LIGHTHOUSE, which cost £60,000, and is erected on a ridge of rocks. It is 168 feet in height, and is painted in bands of black, white and red. The light flashes every ten seconds, and can be seen in clear weather at a distance of eighteen miles.

The visitor should now retrace his steps past the Barracks and Depôt to the junction of the two roads to the north of the latter point, and passing along the one to his left, the Wodehouse Road—will pass the PARSEE SANITARIUM set apart for the accommodation of members of the Zoroastrian religion. The road from this point skirts Back Bay, and on the right will be noticed the buildings erected by the military authorities for the European Staff of the Ordnance Department.

At this point a considerable area of Back Bay has been reclaimed by the City Improvement Trust, to provide sites for future buildings.

The next building possessing architectural interest is the COLABA STATION of the B. B. & C. I. Railway, which occupies a commanding site. It is extremely well designed, and has at its southern end a stone facade and carriage porch. Entering the station, the traveller will find waiting rooms, an open ticket counter, and all the other necessary offices of the station staff conveniently placed. Inside the building are three broad platforms, each some five hundred feet in length, alongside which five lines of metals have been laid, which prove ample for the traffic at the station. The lofty roof has been painted in delicate colours, a feature of the building being that the principal columns and a good deal of the other iron-work have been formed out of old rails. At the south-west corner of the station, opened in 1896, is situated a high tower with a pointed tiled roof.

Following the roadway over the Wodehouse Bridge, constructed in 1875, the new ROMAN CATHOLIC CATHEDRAL will be seen. It has been well designed by Mr. W. A. Chambers and its interior is elaborately decorated with paintings. The facade of the building is surmounted by two lofty towers, and is flanked on either side by the residence of the Bishop and the Convent School. The Elphinstone College Students' quarters will be found located in rear of the above buildings, and a few hundred yards further north the stranger will again arrive at the Wellington Fountain, and so bring his second tour to a close.

Malabar Hill.

—

FEW pleasant [...] be found within the limits of t[...]n that skirting Back Bay and pa[...]labar Hill. Assuming the stranger has elected to visit the latter locality, he should, on leaving the Fort, turn into the Queen's Road at Church Gate Station. Leaving the compact little station on his left and following the thoroughfare named in a northerly direction, he will pass on his right the General's bungalow and others in which are situated the mess-houses of the two Bombay Native Infantry Regiments. The strip of land between the B. B. & C. I. offices and Marine Lines Station, known as the Marine Lines, is covered with some of the best designed residences in the city, many of which are worthy of inspection and the whole standing in well laid out gardens.

Passing the Marine Lines Station, to the left of the railway, will be seen the pavilions and grounds of the Parsee, Mahomedan, and Hindu Gymkhanas in the order named. On the right hand side of the Queen's

MACMILLAN'S BUILDING, HORNBY ROAD.

Road a high wall will be noticed that encloses the Hindu Burning and the Mahomedan Burial Grounds.

Further along will be seen the SONAPORE CEMETERY used for Christian burial up till 1867 when the present cemetery at Sewree was opened. The Sonapore burial ground is now separated from the roadway by a low wall surmounted by an ornamental railing. Among those buried there are Major-General V. Kennedy, President of the Royal Asiatic Society, who died in 1846 ; and Colonel Ford, who commanded a brigade at the battle of Kirkee. The large bungalow at the corner of the Thakurdwar Road is used as a Fire Temple by the Parsees. Passing the Charni Road Garden and the Railway Station on the left, and the Adamjee Peerbhoy Dhuramsala, the latter a long range of two storey buildings, on the right, the visitor will find a short distance up Charni Road the ALLBLESS BAGH, the principal place for the celebration of marriages among Parsees, and which, on the occasion of the nuptials of wealthy Zoroastrians, is brilliantly illuminated.

Crossing the railway lines and still following the roadway round the Bay, after passing a range of attractive residences on the right, the visitor will then reach the WILSON COLLEGE. The institution arose out of an English school for native youths founded by the late Rev. Dr. Wilson in 1832, and was originally dependant on local contributions. It was afterwards recognised in 1835 by the Church of Scotland, and in 1843 by the Free Church of Scotland, from which body it receives the greater part of its funds. In addition to the College Division affiliated

to the University, and preparing students for the
Arts and Science degrees, there is a School Division,
educating up to the matriculation standard of the Bombay University. The college building was erected partly
by subscriptions and by a Government grant. The style
of architecture used is that known as the domestic
gothic Coorla and P⸱   being mainly used
in constructing the b   has a very effective
outline. The spacious   hern end, is provided
with large doors and   is embellished with
a fine gallery. The r   e structure is appropriated to class room   and rooms for the
professors, a wide stai   o the upper floors
from the principal en

Continuing to follo   Road the stranger
will then commence t... ....ALABAR HILL by the
Walkeshwar Road, and on his way will pass on either
hand residences occupied by Europeans or wealthy
Natives. About half way up the hill the private entrance
gate to Government House will be noticed on the left.
At the end of the hill the Walkeshwar Road, at its junction with the Ridge, descends towards the main gates of
the Government House grounds. On entering the latter
a guard-house and stables will be noticed on the left, and
the Malabar Hill North Battery, containing two 10 inch
muzzle-loading guns on the right. GOVERNMENT HOUSE
will be found at the end of the drive, and consists of a
series of bungalows.

Returning to and proceeding along the Ridge Road,
which together with the roads on the left leading down
to the sea front, are thickly populated by the wealthier

residents of the City. Many of the bungalows are well designed, and situated in tastefully laid out grounds, which command fine views over the surrounding country. About 100 yards past the corner of Mount Pleasant and Nepean Roads, the visitor will come to the LADIES' GYMKHANA, which has a large membership, a spacious pavilion, and occupies ground on either side of the road, in which Tennis Courts are laid out. Adjoining the Gymkhana is a Post Office, in rear of which will be found ALL SAINTS' CHURCH.

The next objects of interest to be noticed are the HANGING GARDENS and the RESEVOIR. The latter is on the left of the Ridge, and is surrounded by pleasant walks and flower beds. The Hanging Gardens on the east side of the road are well laid out, the red earth pathways receding down the face of the hill. From the Gardens a splendid view can be obtained over the island, Chowpatty lying at the foot of the hill in the midst of cocoanut trees, while the Fort and Colaba can be seen to the right, and Mazagon, the Mills of Parel and Mahaluxmi noticed stretching away to the north-east.

Leaving the gardens, one of the most delightful spots in Bombay, and descending the Gibbs Road, a stone viaduct will be crossed, under which pass the flight of steps leading to the gates of the enclosure in which are built the TOWERS OF SILENCE. The Towers, five in number, can be reached either by way of the steps from the Gibbs Road or by the private road constructed by the late Sir Jamsetjee Jeejeebhoy, Bart., which leads from the Gowalia Tank Road. Strangers are not allowed to enter the grounds unless provided with a permit from the Secretary of the Parsee Panchayat. The grounds have an area of over seventy-five thousand square yards. On entering them the visitor will notice the stone building set apart for a house of prayer and the fire temple. The Towers of Silence, the largest of which measures 276 feet in circumference, are all surrounded by high wall   ity-five feet in height, and have an opening   ad-level, though which the dead bodies are (corpse-bearers are the only persons allowed   e towers, but there is an excellent model   nds, which is generally shown to visitors.)   nd that bodies of the deceased are laid in g   id the well, which is to be found in the cen   tower. The bodies of young children are   centre circle, those of females in the second   of the men in the outer ring. The bodies, after being exposed in this manner, are in a short time stripped of flesh by numerous vultures that are always to be found in the vicinity, and then the bones are thrown into the well, where they are allowed to decompose.

Turning sharp to the left at Messrs. Kemp's shop, on the right will be found the massive building known as the FRAMJEE DINSHAW PETIT SANITARIUM. The building, which was opened by Lord Northcote in 1902, is 227 feet in length, its average depth being 75 feet. It consists of two upper floors, and provides accommodation for thirty-six families in all, twelve on each floor. Each family is provided with one sitting-room (14ft. by 17ft.), and bed-room (14ft. by 17ft.), with a dining verandah in the rear. There are two towers at each end of the

THE KING'S STATUE.

ELPHINSTONE COLLEGE.

building, facing the road. Over the carriage porch is a medallion containing the marble bust of the late Mr. Framjee Petit. Following the Warden Road to the right at the foot of the hill, the MAHALUXMI BATTERY will be passed, and, being comparatively open, the stranger will be able to view specimens of the heavy ordnance used in the several forts round the island. Adjacent to the Battery is the BEACH CANDY SWIMMING BATHS for Europeans, built out of the proceeds of a fund raised for the purpose of chartering passenger steamers to and from Aden previous to the P. & O. Company running through steamers to Bombay.

About half-a-mile further on the MAHALUXMI TEMPLE and TANK will be observed, and if he still follows the road for another quarter of a mile the stranger will reach a point where three roads divide. The crescent shaped road to the left is known as HORNBY'S VELLARD, and was built by the Governor of that name about 1770-80. By its construction all the low-lying land to the north and east was reclaimed from the sea. The Vellard, which has rows of trees planted throughout its length, is a good deal resorted to in the evenings by those desirous of enjoying the sea breeze. The road to the right of the Vellard leads across the "Flats" to Jacob's Circle, Byculla and Parel; but leaving those districts for a subsequent visit, the stranger should follow the right hand or Tardeo Road on his way back to the Fort. Passing the Alliance and Manockji Petit Mills and then bearing to his right he will come to the corner of the Grant Road. Leaving Grant Road Station and the bridge crossing the railway to his left, he should take the

F

next turning in the same direction, and cross the
Kennedy Bridge. From this point he can either turn
sharp round to his right and follow the Queen's Road
back to the Fort, or continue his journey along the
Girgaum Road. The houses on the latter thoroughfare
are principally tenanted by Parsees, which community
has built a large Fire Temple at the southern end of the
road, in the Dh   t. The roadway ter-
minates at the M
should proceed t   of the Esplanade
Road.

Byculla and Mazagon.

HAVING become acquainted with the principal objects of interest to the south and west of the island, the stranger for his fourth journey cannot do better than elect to make a tour through the Byculla and Mazagon districts. In doing so he should proceed to the Money School by way of the Esplanade Road. Thence traversing the Kalbadevie Road and passing a large Hindoo Temple on his right, at the corner of Bhuleshwar road will be seen the Municipal Markets and School buildings which consist of a ground floor and two upper storeys. The market occupies the whole of the ground floor. It consists of 170 stalls exclusively set apart for the sale of fruit and vegetables. The school rooms on the upper floors form three sides of a rectangle.

Arriving at Pydownie after a journey through a densely populated thoroughfare, he will pass several Hindoo Temples, the Coppersmiths' Bazaar, the Mombadavie Temple and Tank, and the Goldsmiths' Bazaar,

where may be purchased rings, bangles, and other articles
of jewellery of native workmanship.   Leaving Pydownie
and following the Parel Road northwards, after passing
the Jain Temple on the right and a small Mahomedan
Mosque on the left, if the sightseer on reaching the Jail
Road turns to his right and proceeds along it he will
pass the MAHOMEDAN IMAMBARA, having a lofty gateway
flanked by two domed towers, in which during the
Mohurrum tragic portrayal of the murder of Hoosein
and Hassan takes place yearly.   Further along the road
will be found the COMMON JAIL.

Retracing his steps to, and continuing his journey
along the Parel Road, the large compound in which are
situated the Sir Jamsetjee Jeejeebhoy Hospital and Grant
Medical College, &c., will be found on the right at the
corner of the Baboola Tank Road.   The GRANT MEDICAL
COLLEGE, with its Laboratory, is near the roadway.
The College was established in the year 1845, as a tribute
to the memory of the late Sir Robert Grant, Governor of
Bombay.   The object of its establishment is to impart the
benefits of medical instruction to the natives of Western
India.   A moiety of the cost of the building was defrayed by the friends of Sir Robert Grant and the remainder
by Government, who also provide the funds for the support of the College, with the exception of certain endowments for the encouragement of deserving students.

The entrance to the JAMSETJEE JEEJEEBHOY HOSPITAL
is in the Baboola Tank Road.   The building was opened
in May 1845, having been erected at the joint expense
of the East India Company and the late Sir Jamsetjee
Jeejeebhoy for the relief of the native sick poor of all classes

THE DOCKS.—OFFICES AND ENTRANCE GATES.

for whose accommodation there are over 500 beds,
Further along the road is the entrance to two more
charitable institutions, namely, the BAI MOTLABAI HOS-
PITAL and the SIR DINSHAW MANOCKJEE PETIT HOSPI-
TAL. The former, is an Obstetric Hospital, of which
the foundation stone was laid by Lord Reay on the
9th March, 1889. The building is 163 feet in length
by 48 feet in breadth. On either side of the
entrance hall stretch verandahs, doors from which lead
into four wards, affording accommodation for ten beds.
At the north end is an operating room. In the rear are
nurses' quarters. The first floor is similarly planned,
there being four wards capable of holding ten beds,
making a total accommodation for twenty patients in the
whole Hospital. The foundation-stone of the SIR
DINSHAW MANOCKJEE PETIT HOSPITAL for women and
children was laid by Lord Reay on the 27th January,
1890. The building is 127 feet in length by 48 feet in
width.

On again returning to the Parel Road and following
that thoroughfare northwards the JEWISH SYNAGOGUE will
be passed on the left, opposite which, at the corner of
Nesbit Road, is the G. I. P. Railway infirmary. A short
distance down Nesbit Road is the ST. MARY'S COLLEGE.
The school and college is conducted by Roman
Catholic priests. The Institution consists of two large
buildings : the Boarding School, a three storied house
(22 × 40 feet), and a two-storied School-house (260 ×
32 feet). There are two well ventilated dormitories
(160 × 40 and 156 + 32), two large study-rooms, two
dining-rooms, two libraries and a spacious lavatory.

There is a spacious compound in rear of the building,
the St. Ann's Church being situated at its western end.
Its object is to provide Catholic youths with a liberal and
sound education, to train them in Christian virtues and
thus prepare them for their future career in life. The
Institution consists of a High School, for Europeans, and
an English-teaching School. Both Schools have their
own separate class-rooms, 15 in number, and their own
separate staff of teachers, of whom two-thirds are members of the Society of Jesus. The course of instruction
comprises all the subjects required by Government for
the Standards of European high schools in the Bombay
Presidency. The physical training of the pupils is
provided for, not only by the common games and sports
in their spacious play-grounds and sheds, but also by
systematic drilling and gymnastics. The college turns
out a strong company of cadets, and a band which is
amalgamated with the Bombay Volunteer Rifle Corps.
In the hot months the boys are taken up to Khandalla,
where there is a branch of the institution.

Further along Parel road in a large compound are the
schools of the Bombay Education Society. The institution was founded in 1815 by the exertions of the
Venerable Archdeacon Barnes, and has for its object
the training up of the children of Europeans in
the principles of Christianity, and teaching them such
knowledge and habits of industry as may render them
useful members of the community. In 1825 the school
was removed from the Fort to Byculla. The land for
this purpose was a free grant from Government, and
the present buildings, accommodating 150 boys and a

similar number of girls, were erected at a cost of Rs. 1,71,238. Day scholars are received in addition. The children belong to two distinct classes—orphans who are entirely supported by the funds of the Society, and orphans belonging to the " Military Asylum," the cost of whose support is defrayed by Government. There is a Printing Press in connection with the Society, the profits from which may be said to be the mainstay of the school, which nevertheless is greatly dependent on the charitable public for its support. In the same compound is CHRIST CHURCH, a commodious and well designed place of worship.

On the foot of Byculla bridge and at the corner of Sankli Street is the head office and station of the Municipal Fire Brigade.

In the Clare Road which joins the Parel Road at this point will be found the ST. ELIZABETH'S HOME. The institution is intended for European widows and respectable ladies in need of a home, they being admitted as boarders. There is a school for girls and children connected with the institution, which is admirably managed by the nuns of Jesus and Mary. The HOUSE OF CORRECTION and Government Workhouse are also situated on the east side of the latter road.

The BYCULLA CLUB house founded in 1833, is situated in spacious grounds on Bellasis Road and is the most influential of the many clubs in the city.

Immediately after crossing Byculla Bridge the school house of the Scottish Education Society will be found at the corner of Love Lane. The STRANGERS' HOME is also in Love Lane. It was established in 1863 for the relief of

destitute Europeans, and to extinguish European vagran-
cy. Inmates of the home are expected to search diligently
for work, the Society, so far as it is able, assisting them
in this respect.   The Home is supported by an Endow-
ment Fund and a Government grant, supplemented by
contributions from the public.

About a quarter of a mile further along the Parel
Road, the entrance to the Byculla railway station,
and the Tramway stables will be noticed.   Opposite the
latter are the VICTORIA GARDENS, [which during recent
years have been extensively remodelled, and will now
amply repay the trouble of a drive from the Fort.   They
cover an area of over thirty-five acres, and are in charge
of the Municipality, whose superintendent has brought
them up to a high state of perfection.   The grounds are
well laid out, a number of broad paths leading in all
directions between the flower-beds.   The gardens, to be
seen at their best, should be visited either during the early
morning or evening.   A handsome clock tower, the gift
of the Sassoons, is erected near the entrance gates.   In
the grounds there is a zoological collection, the animals for
the most part being housed in cages presented by some
of the wealthier citizens or public bodies of Bombay.
The gardens are open free daily.   The VICTORIA AND
ALBERT MUSEUM is located to the left of the main
entrance, and has been established for the purpose of
exhibiting the raw products and manufactures of India
and for illustrating the processses of important manufactures.   It was originally called the Government
Central Museum, and was located in the Town Hall.
In 1858 a meeting of the European and native inhabitants

PRINCE'S DOCK.—THE JETTY.

of Bombay was held to establish a museum in commemoration of the suppression of the Mutiny. Lord Elphinstone, the then Governor, finding the residents readily subscribing large sums for the erection of a suitable building, communicated to Queen Victoria the resolutions passed by the meeting, when the late Queen suggested that the Institution be called the " Victoria and Albert Museum." The Museum now contains raw products, minerals, manufactures, illustrations of some of the manufactures of the Presidency, and natural history specimens, and is open to the public on week-days, Wednesdays excepted, from 10-30 a.m. to 5-30 p.m.; and on Sundays from 7 a.m. to 10 a.m., and 2 p.m., to 6 p.m. Admission free.

After leaving the gardens the lofty central tower of the VICTORIA JUBILEE TECHNICAL INSTITUTE building forms a prominent object. The Institute was established in 1887, in commemoration of Queen Victoria's Jubilee, and is located in a handsome building, the gift of Sir Dinshaw Manockjee Petit. Science and Art classes meet during the day and evening ; the object of the Society being to train persons of either sex in the industrial arts, grants being received from Government, the Municipality, and millowners.

The tour northwards may now be brought to a close at this point, and the visitor, in order to return to the Fort by way of the Mazagon district, should retrace his steps along the Parel Road towards Byculla Bridge. Turning down the Victoria Road, the first turning to the left after repassing the gardens, he should on reaching the far end of that thoroughfare proceed to

his right along the Mount Road. Providing the stranger
does so, he will next observe on his right hand AGA
KHAN'S MAUSOLEUM, an imposing edifice capped with
numerous golden domes. Passing the tramway terminus
and following the car tracks the tourist should turn to his
left at the Dockyard Road. If he follows the windings
of the latter he w   o the ST. PETER'S
SCHOOLS. The larg   l buildings for boys
and girls are buil   ygrounds and the
excellent teaching   owley, Fathers and
Sisters of the All S   s rendered them a
credit to Mazagon.   eater proportion of
of the boarders hav   Khandalla where a
new hill school has

A few hundred y   Dockyard Road is
ST. PETER'S CHURC   le funds bequeathed
by a resident of the district named Shephard. The
church is capable of seating about 250 persons, and
contains a memorial window to those who were drowned
in the P. & O. Steamer "Carnatic." Its site has been
acquired for new Port Trust railway to Sion, but it is
projected to rebuild the Church in the neighbourhood.
Further along the road towards Mazagon Bunder, in
former years the landing place for mail steamer passengers during the monsoon, will be found the massive
entrance gates to the P. & O. DOCKYARD. The company's property is surrounded by a high wall within
which are steam factories and workshops capable of
turning out machinery for and repairing the vessels
of the P. & O. fleet that visit the port.

Returning to the St. Peter's Schools and proceeding
south along De Lima Street, the Wari Bunder Goods

station and sidings of the G. I. P. Railway will be passed. The station covers a very extensive area and during the grain season is exceptionally busy, the yards being stacked with bags of grain brought down from up-country for shipment, which are either taken to the adjacent docks by bullock cart, or conveyed alongside the vessels in railway wagons. At this point the stranger will enter upon the Frere Road, one of the longest and straightest thoroughfares in the city, and which passes through the centre of the busy portion of the town in the vicinity of the docks.

The Dock Traffic Office is centrally placed between the entrances to the Prince's and Victoria docks, and is provided with a large turret containing a clock and surmounted by a time-ball that falls daily at noon. The Traffic Office was commenced in January 1888, and completed in June 1890. It is a handsome and substantial building, somewhat Italian in style, of local basalt with facings of Coorla stone, the light yellow tint of the latter contrasting most pleasantly with the deep blue of the former. The building is three storeys high, with the ground-floor 142 feet in length and 89 feet in breadth, 53 feet high to the top cornice, and 140 feet to the top of the vane of the time-ball mast. On the north side are located the offices of the Dock Superintendent and his departmental staff officers, while on the south side are the Traffic Manager and his staff; these take up the ground and the first floor, while on the top flat there are the audit offices and the quarters of the Dock Master. Adjoining and to the south of the office a New Customs House is in course of erection. Entering the Docks

through the gates to the left of the offices, it will be
noticed that boards placed on the jetty sheds indicate
the berths allotted to all the principal lines of steamers.·

The first stone of the PRINCE'S DOCK was laid by the
Prince of Wales on November 11th, 1875, the dock,
which cost nearly Rs. 68,00,000, being opened for
traffic on New Year's day 1880. It has a water area of 30
acres, and is 1,460 feet in length by 1,000 feet wide with
a jetty at the north end 700 feet by 240 feet. The two
water gates are respectively 66 and 55 feet wide, the
depth of water on the sill at ordinary spring tides being
28 feet, the bottom of the dock being excavated 3 feet
below that depth. The dock, which is capable of
berthing about 16 vessels, has a quayage of 6,049 feet
inside and 1,590 feet on the harbour side. There
are forty-seven movable 30 cwt. hydraulic cargo cranes
on the wharves, and one 30 ton crane at the head of
the jetty. There are 11 closed sheds with a combined
length of 2,340 feet and a jetty shed 480 by 158 feet.

The VICTORIA DOCK, which was opened in March
1888, is 1,270 feet long by 1,000 feet wide, and has a
water area of 25 acres, and length of quays equal to
7,200 feet, affording accommodation for 16 steamers.
The communication passage leading to the Prince's
Dock is 64 feet wide, and the massive single entrance
gate from the harbour 80 feet in width. There is a
depth of 30 feet of water on the sill, the dock being
excavated 3 feet below that measurement. The dock has
three jetties on the west side, the " Ibis " crane, capable
of raising 100 tons, being fixed at the end of the south
jetty. There is also a 20-ton crane, and fifty-five 30

PRINCE'S DOCK.—ENTRANCE GATES.

cwt. cranes in the dock, which is completely fitted with hydraulic machinery.

The MEREWETHER DRY DOCK, situated at the north-west corner of the Prince's dock, is 550 feet long and has an entrance of 65½ feet. It is capable of receiving the largest man-of-war or merchant vessel visiting the port.

Facing the central gates of the docks is ST. NICHOLAS CHURCH, and the SEAMEN'S INSTITUTE, and a few yards further down, and on the opposite side of the road, the SEAMEN'S REST. Passing the end of the Carnac Road, Carnac Bunder, the starting point of Messrs. Shepherd & Co.'s Goa and Cutch Coasting steamers, will be found to the left. Extending southward for a considerable distance on the right is the Carnac Bunder Goods Station of the B. B. & C. I. Railway. Nearly opposite the southern extremity of the goods yard is the Frere Road Dhuramsala, a red brick building. Passing the rear of St. George's Hospital, part of old Fort St. George will be seen, the walls of the ruins, the only portion of the ancient outworks of the city, being loop-holed for rifle fire. Having glanced at the massive oil tanks belonging to the Bulk Oil Installations to the left of the road, the visitor can then proceed directly south to his hotel by way of the Mint Road.

Parel and ı ı Suburbs.

TO reach Parel, d travel over the B. B. & C. Elphinstone Road Station. Just before ı nation he will pass on his left the extensiv. kshops and Locomotive Depôt of the Railway. Leaving the station and driving eastward over the level crossings, the CHURCH OF THE HOLY CROSS will be noticed on the right. The Parel Convent is on the Dadur Road, and the entrance to the G. I. P. Railway Works on the Supari Bagh Road. Crossing the end of both thoroughfares the visitor will then come to the gates of the OLD GOVERNMENT HOUSE. Originally a Portuguese Church, the building, in the middle of the eighteenth century, was purchased by Government and additions made to it. For several years past the Governors of Bombay have ceased to reside at Parel.

Leaving the grounds by the south gate, the high ornamental gateway of the VETERINARY COLLEGE will be seen. The College has been established by Government on an estate presented by the late Sir Dinshaw Manock-jee Petit, and is worked in conjunction with the Bai Sa-karbai Dinshaw Petit Hospital for Animals of the Bombay Society for the Prevention of Cruelty to Animals, the Veterinary Officers of the College being *ex-officio* in charge of the latter hospital. The special objects of the College are to train competent practitioners for veterinary service under Government, for private practice, for service in Native States, and for special posts under Municipalities, District Local Boards, etc.

At the rear of Government House, and approached by way of Parel Village, is SEWREE CEMETERY. Situated in what were formerly the old Botanical Gardens, it now forms the only place in the Island for the burial of Europeans. The well-kept churchyard nestles in a valley between two hills. The Cemetery contains many handsome monuments.

At Matoonga, some two miles north of Parel, is the LEPER ASYLUM, which contains six wards. The inmates are well cared for, and instead of living the lives of outcasts in misery, beggary, and much bodily pain, are well housed, well treated, and their sufferings alleviated to a remarkable degree.

Further north Sion Causeway will be noticed. A fine stretch of backwater runs along the north of the island from the causeway to that connecting Mahim with Bandora.

BANDORA, although not strictly within the island, is a favourite place of residence for many business men of Bombay, who have their bungalows on the hill. The railway station is an ornamental building. The St. Joseph's

Convent and St. Stanislaus Institution are worth a visit. The meat-supply of the City passes through the slaughter-houses here.

Turning south along the Causeway and the Mahim Lower Road, the SCOTTISH ORPHANAGE will be found on the left, pleasantly situated in the Mahim woods. The building was opened on the 13th April, 1878, by H. E. Sir Richard Temple. There are about 100 children of both sexes resident in the Orphanage, which is dependent on the public to a considerable extent for support. The Orphanage had its origin in an institution established in 1847, primarly for the benefit of the daughters of the Presbyterian soldiers and Indian Navy Seamen, called the "Scottish Female Orphanage." In 1857 a similar institution was established for boys. In 1859 the two Orphanages were united under the name of "The Bombay Presbyterian Male and Female Orphanage," and four years later that name was altered to the one the institution now bears. Following the roadway south, the stranger should, after having taken a stroll on the neighbouring sandy beach lying between Mahim and Worli points, bear to his left to the railway stations at Dadur or Elphinstone Road, and return thence by train to the city.

It may be stated that at Mahim and Worli there are old Portuguese forts, the latter of which, approached by way of Worli village, is in ruins and somewhat interesting. There are other similar old forts at Rowli, Sion and Sewree, on the northern and eastern sides of the island.

VIEW IN VICTORIA GARDENS.

Places of Interest near Bombay.

ELEPHANTA CAVES.—Visitors can proceed from the Apollo Bunder to Elephanta Island during the fair season by steam launch or sailing boat. Elephanta, called by the natives Gharapuri, the town of excavation, is an island 7 miles from Bombay. Elephanta, the European name, was given to the island by the Portuguese in honour of a huge rock-cut elephant, now in the Victoria Gardens, that stood on a knoll a little to the east of the village. On landing, after passing over a pier of concrete blocks, and mounting a flight of steps, a terrace is reached, which commands a fine view of sea and mountain, and leads to the front of the cave. The cave forms two parts, a central hall about ninety feet square, and four aisles or vestibules, each sixteen feet deep, and fifty-four feet long. It rests on 26 pillars (eight of them now broken) and 16 pilasters. As neither floor nor roof of the cave is level, the pillars vary in height from fifteen to seventeen feet. They are strong, massive, and of considerable elegance. The chief object which attracts the visitors is the colossal three-headed bust that faces him on the

3

south wall. The bust represents Shiv, who is the leading character in all of the groups of the cave. The
expression of the central face, representing Shiv in the
character of Brahma the creator, is mild and peaceful.
In his left hand Brahma holds a citron. The right hand
is broken. The breast is adorned with a necklace of
large stones or p‌   it is a deep richly-
wrought breast or‌   ‌er border is festoon-
ed perhaps with p‌   dress consists of the
hair raised in the   with, on the top of
the hair, a royal   ‌tifully carved. The
face to the left is   the destroyer. The
brow has an oval s   ‌e nose, representing
a third eye. Tl   ‌stern, commanding
expression. He i‌   ‌ra which is twisted
round his arm, an   hood looks him in
the face. Among his ornaments are some of the pecu-
liar symbols of Shiv—a human skull over the temple ; a
leaf of the *Gloriosa Superba*, a branch apparently of the
milk-brush ; twisted snakes instead of hair, and high
up a cobra erect with outstretched hood. The right
face has generally been considered to be Shiv in the
character of Vishnu the preserver holding a lotus flower
in his hand. The face is gentle and placid. The figures
at the portals are Hindu door-keepers.

In the compartment to the visitor's left, or east of
the Triumvira, there is a gigantic four-armed half male
half-female figure representing Ardhanareshvar—that is
the God which combines the active or manlike, that is,
Shiv, and the passive or womanlike,—that is, Uma,
principles in nature. This figure, which is sixteen feet

nine inches high, leans to the right, or male side, and
rests on the bull *nandi* with one of its forearms. The
right side has a crescent which, as well as the cobra
with outstretched hood, was a symbol of the Ling worship. The male arm holds a mirror and the female a
mirror. On the right of the figure is Brahma on his
lotus throne supported by five servants. Three of his
four faces are visible. A little nearer to Shiv is Indra,
Lord of the Firmament, riding on the heavenly elephant. In his left hand he carries the thunderbolt.
On the other side of Shiva Vishnu is seen riding on his
carrier, the half man, half eagle, called Garud. In the
compartment on the visitor's right are two gigantic
figures of Shiv and Parvati. Shiv has a high cap on
which are sculptured the crescent and the other emblems, and from it rises a cup, or shell, in which is a
singular three-headed female figure representing the
three sacred rivers—Ganges, Jumna, and Saresvati.
According to Hindu legend, the Ganges flowed from
the head of Shiv. On Shiv's left stands Parvati in a
graceful attitude. On Shiv's right are Brahma and
Indra ; on Parvatis left is Vishnu on Garud.

To the west of the cave is a square chamber with
four doors facing the cardinal points. In the centre of
the chamber is the Ling or large conical stone intended
to represent the prolific power of nature. This is the
most sacred object in the cave. Around the chapel, on
the outside, are a number of large figures representing
door-keepers.

To the west of Shiv is the western aisle, and the
group in the south wall of this portico represents the

marriage of Shiv and Parvati. The figure of Parvati is one of the best proportioned in the cave. Facing the marriage scene is one of the most remarkable sculptures in the cave. The main figure represents Shiv in the terrible form he assumed when he heard from his first wife Sita that he was not asked to a sacrifice given by her father. The face is charged with passion. Over the left shoulder an   h hangs a rosary of human heads. Coi   the west and after crossing a courtyar   come to a chamber with another Ling.   this shrine contains a good deal of sculj   ntre is Shiv, seated as an ascetic on a l   -entering the great cave and passing (st wing, the visitor will come upon a c   hich Shiv and Parvati are seated toge   of male and female divinities showerin   from above. The rock is cut into various snapes to represent the clouds that rest on the summits of Karlas. Behind Shiv and Parvati is a female figure carrying a child on her hip from which it has been supposed that the face represents the birth of Ganesha or Gunpati, afterwards the elephant-headed god of wisdom. If the visitor now faces completely round and walks a few steps he will come to a compartment in which is represented the attempt of Ravan, the demon King of Ceylon, to remove Karlas, the heavenly mountain. Ravan has ten heads and arms, and is with his back to the spectator. Shiv with eight arms is seen by Karlas, with Parvati on his right and votaries in the background.

In order to get to the east wing the visitor must descend a few steps and cross a courtyard. He will then come to some steps, on each side of which are stone tigers or leogriffs. In the centre of the east wing is a Ling-shrine. At the south end is a larger image of Ganesh. The west wall is nearly filled with a row of ten colossal figures standing on a base about two feet high. Most of the figures are badly defaced.

Besides the great cave there are four other caves in the island : two are on the same ridge as the one out of which the great cave is excavated, the other two being on the opposite ridge, and approached only by a path through the jungle.

BASSEIN.—To reach Bassein, which is now little better than a city of ruins, the traveller should proceed by B. B. & C. I. Railway to Bassein Road station. In 1534 the city was ceded to the Portuguese, and for more than two centuries it remained in their possession and rose to great prosperity under their rule, many noble buildings being erected. In 1739 it was besieged by the Mahrattas, and after a brave resistance captured by them, though they did not long keep possession, for in 1780 it was re-captured by the British. Two years afterwards, by the treaty of Salbai, it was restored to the Mahrattas, and in 1818, on the overthrow of the Peshwa, it was resumed by the English. The objects of interest are the Cathedral of St. Joseph and the ruined citadel. Inside the gate the whole place is strewn with ruins. To the left are the ruins of a bastion with the oldest inscription in Bassein. Behind the bastion are the ruined palaces of the General of the North and the Captain of Bassein. In the garden of the General of the North's palace are the Church and Hospital of Pity. Parallel to this is the Church of *Nossa Senhora da Vida.* In the front of the square are ruins of the church and monastery of the Jesuits, the foundation of which was laid in 1543. A little beyond these ruins is the Franciscan Church of the Invocation of St. Antonio, the oldest and one ligious buildings in Bassein. It was he is Xavier is said to have stayed during between 1544 and 1548. To the rig scan ruins are the ruins of the Domin lt in 1583.

VEHAR LAKE is c ing grounds for the Bombay water-sup e of storing a depth of 59 feet of water, f 1,400 acres. The dam, which is 84 vas constructed in 1856-58. Other lakes have been formed at Tulsi in 1885, at Powai in 1890, and at Tansa, distance 51 miles from Bombay, in order to increase the water-supply of the city. Vehar Lake can be reached from Coorla (7 miles), and Tansa from Atgaon, on the G. I. P. Railway.

TANNA.—The ancient Portuguese fort, now used as the jail, is worth a visit. It is calculated to accommodate one thousand convicts, who are employed manufacturing carpets, drills and other cloths, and basket-work. In the churchyard of St. James' Protestant Church are interred the Chiefs of Salsette and many officers of the garrison, when Tanna, at the beginning of this century, formed the northern boundary to the British Indian possessions. The Roman Catholic Cathedral stands on the banks of a picturesque lake. It was built in 1609.

KENNERY CAVES.—To Tanna by G. I. P. Railway, thence 6 miles or to Borivli by B. B. & C. I. Railway, and thence 3 miles. These caves are all excavated in the face of a single hill. There are 109 of them ; but though more numerous, are much less interesting than those at Karli. The great cave is 88½ feet long by 38½ broad, with a vaulted nave 40 feet high resting on 34 octagonal pillars. The Durbar cave is 96½ feet by 42¼ feet, but only 9 feet high. Traces of painting can be seen in nearly all the caves. From the top of the hill there is a splendid view of Bombay city and harbour.

IGATPURI.—Is a sanitarium situated at the top of the Thull Ghaut of the G. I. P. Railway, nearly two thousand feet above the level of the sea, and is frequented by European visitors during the hot season, the air being cool and invigorating. There are good and well wooded camping grounds on elevated sites. The Railway Company have locomotive works at Igatpuri, in which they employ a large number of Europeans and natives. There is a Church of England, and also Methodist and Roman Catholic churches and schools, an Institute, a Masonic Lodge, and a Co-operative Store. Boating can be had on the lake which supplies the town with water. There is a refreshment-room the station and a Dâk Bungalow a short distance away.

NASIK.—The city of Nasik, about 5 miles from the Nasik Road Station of the G. I. P. Railway, contains a Travellers' Bungalow. Tongas can be obtained at the railway station. The city, which is very ancient, and considered sacred by the Hindus, is situated on the river Godavery. The river bank is studded with Hindu temples. The climate is very healthy and soil fertile. Gungapur, six miles distant. on the banks of the Godavery, contains 9 temples and a pretty waterfall, Trimbak, distant 20 miles, at the source of the Godavery, is also considered sacred by the Hindus. This village, as also the town of]　　　　　by vast numbers of pilgrims once in eve　　　　　Nasik is the headquarters of the Coll(　　　　　.ena Caves, 5 miles from Nasik on the :　　　　　worthy of a visit. The Church Missio　　　　　nt at Sharanpur is about a mile and ;　　　　　city. Sir George Campbell, in consid　　　　　esirable seat for the Viceregal Governn　　　　　nt of Calcutta and Simla being aband　　　　　Nasik as offering the greatest adv　　　　　int of position, climate, &c. Its average rainfall is 35 inches. Height above sea level about 1,900 feet. It has been said that Nasik derives its temperate climate from its proximity to the sea, being only about 60 miles from Bulsar, the fresh breezes from which find their way through the Peiet gorges. Nasik is noted for an extensive trade in copper and brass wares.

MATHERAN.—From the Victoria Terminus by G. I. P. Railway to Neral Station whence the road up the hill, though broad enough for two ponies, is unfit for carriages or carts, passes south through Neral village for about a mile to the foot of the hill. During the second mile the hill-side in places is cut into the rock, winds about 550 feet up the western face of the spur, and during the third mile rises to about 1,000 feet, the road leaving the plateau and climbing a rugged hill-side strewn with boulders and with lines of coarse withered grass, dry underwood, and bare, leafless trees. Close to the fourth mile, at a height of 1,525 feet, the road enters the sheltered bit of the Neral wood with varied lines of green and sprinkling of leafless grey. The end of the fifth mile brings the traveller to a height of upwards of 2,000 feet. A little beyond the mile-mark stands the hill on the crest of the neck between the high headlands of Governor's Hill to the north and Garbat Hill to the south. The hill-top, which has an estimated area of 5,000 acres, or about eight square miles, consists of a main central block and two smaller side ridges or wings. The central block, with an average breadth of about half a mile, stretches nearly north and south from the narrow ridge of Hart Point in the north to Chauk in the south. Parallel with the main hill, and joined to it by short necks, are two spurs, the larger to the east, stretching about two and a half miles from Panorama Point in the north to Garbat in the south, and the smaller to the west, stretching about a mile and a half from the sharp point of Porcupine to the large bluff of Louisa Point. From the hill the east wing runs north for about a mile and a quarter to the crest of Governor's Hill, and beyond to Panorama Point. South of the hill a spur runs for nearly a mile to Garbat Point. The Church stands on one of the highest and most central sites on the hill, a little north of the Superintendent's residence. The foundation was laid in 1858, and with the help of a Government grant was completed by private subscriptions in 1861 at a

cost of Rs. 26,260, and consecrated by Bishop Harding
in 1865. It is a plain, neat building, with seats for 130
persons, and has a richly painted window, the gift of
the late Mr. Michael Scott. The Catholic Chapel of
the Holy Cross is situated near the Superintendent's
office, and has seats for ninety people. The Library is
a small room close to the same office. It has about 500
volumes, and takes the Bombay daily papers and some
of the English papers. The rates of subscription are
Rs. 2 a week, Rs. 3 a fortnight, Rs. 5 a month, and
Rs. 10 a year. The Gymkhana is situated on a small
plateau below and to the north-west of Artist Point.
Round the small circular pavilion are laid out lawn-
tennis and badminton courts and on a terrace to the
south, under a shed, are other badminton courts.
The rates of subscription and rules can be ascertained by
writing to the Superintendent. The Superintendent's,
the post, and the telegraph offices are in one building on
the main road near the Clarendon Hotel.

The principal points of interest, from many of which
splendid views can be obtained, are Panorama Point,
Governor's Hill, Garbat, Alexander, Echo, Landscape,
Louisa, Porcupine, Monkey and Hart Bottle, Monkey
and Chouk Points, and Charlotte Lake. Pleasant
excursions on foot can be made to the hill forts, of Peb
and Prabel, distant about twelve miles.

There are several good hotels at Matheran and a
refreshment-room at Neral Railway Station. The
following is the scale of charges for conveyance between
Neral and Matheran :—

1. For a Palkee or Tonjon with 12 bearers, Rs. 8.

2. For Wallace's Canvas Chair or Munchill with 6 bearers, Rs. 5.

3. For Jinricshaw with 5 bearers between, Rs. 8 to 10.

N. B.—Half charges are made for conveyances order-ed but not used.

on both ghauts, up which the trains are hauled by specially constructed engines, slip sidings being built at intervals to prevent the trains running down the inclines in the event of the train staff losing control.

KHANDALLA.—On the G. I. P. Railway, is a sanitarium 2,000 feet above   nts many attractions to the sportsman   alf a mile from the station is a fine v   mate in the summer is cool, and in C   mber can hardly be surpassed. Ther   ent home and hotels in the station.

LANOWLI.—Th: ; situated at the top of the Bhore Gh   ; G. I. P. Railway. There are extei   rks, Protestant and Roman Catholic (y School, and Institute, a Masonic Lodge, and a Co-operative Store. The station is much visited by Europeans during the hot season, and is well provided with bungalows and hotels. Lanowli Woods, to the right of the station, are a favourite camping ground and picnic resort. Some of the curious shaped trees in the wood are worth notice. A good road leads through the wood to a large lake some two miles distant and to Sakar Pathar, a famous shooting ground about eight miles off. Karli Caves are easily accessible. Soharghar, six miles away, is a hill fort formerly used as a state prison by the Peishwas. There are a temple and mosque within the fort.

KARLI CAVES.—The traveller will find it most convenient to proceed from Lanowli to these caves. Karli cave is certainly the largest as well as the most complete

Chaitya cave hitherto discovered in India. It resembles to a very great extent an early Christian church in its arrangements, consisting of a nave and side aisles, terminating in an apse or semi-dome round which the aisle is carried. The general dimensions of the interior are 126 feet from the entrance to back walls, by 45 feet 7 inches in width.

POONA is the capital of the Deccan and headquarters of the Bombay Army and seat of the Bombay Government during the monsoon months. The climate is temperate, and from June to September like an English spring. Height above sea-level 1,850 feet; average rainfall 35 inches. When the Peishwas became supreme in the Mahratta confederacy, the chief seat of government was removed from Sattara to Poona. After the deposition of the Peishwa Baji Rao (1818) the city became the head-quarters of a British district. It is still of considerable commercial importance, and is famous for manufacture of silver and gold jewellery, and of clay figures representing the natives of India.

The principal places of interest are :—

Albert Edward Institute, in East Street, contains a library of about 1,000 volumes, and was built in commemoration of the visit of the King, then the Prince of Wales. The building cost Rs. 15,000, and was opened in 1880.

Bund Gardens, opened in 1869, on the completion of the Fitzgerald bridge over the Mutha Mula river. The grounds are well laid out, the lower terrace overlooking the river and the Sir Jamsetjee Bund. There is an ornamental fountain and a bandstand. Military bands play here during certain evenings, the gardens being the favourite resort of Poona society.

Council Hall, which was completed in 1870, cost Rs. 1,22,943. It is a building of two floors in the Venetian Gothic style, ' '' ʹ ' ' ʹ :k. On the ground floor is the Counc   y 40 feet by 40 feet, which is surround   s by a gallery. At the south end of   o rooms containing numerous portrai·   :es and nobles, over these rooms being   apart for the use of the Governor.

Deccan Colleg·   style of architecture, and is situated be   Kirkee. Sir Jamsetjee Jeejeebhoy ·   ·,45,963 towards the total cost of its construction, Rs. 1,25,000. It is a double storeyed building covering three sides of a square with a tower 106 feet in height at its north-west corner. The two wings are set apart for students' quarters, the main building containing the class rooms, the large college, hall measuring 70 feet by 25 feet, being on the upper floor.

St. Mary's Church, the oldest in Poona, is situated near the Wanowrie barracks. The military attend this church, which is capable of seating 800 worshippers. St. Paul's Church, near the post office, contains accommodation for 250 persons. St. Patrick's Church (R. C.) is on the east of the General Parade ground, and is a very handsome edifice, capable of seating about 1,000 people.

Sassoon Hospital was completed in 1867, the late David Sassoon contributing Rs. 1,88,000 of the total cost of construction, namely, Rs. 3,10,060. The building, which is in the English Gothic style, has accommodation for 144 patients.

Science College; on the road between Poona and Kirkee, cost Rs. 1,81,647, and was opened in 1869. The building is erected nearly in the form of a square, and has a tower at its north-west corner. It contains a large central hall, lecture-room, numerous class-rooms and a museum. Attached are workshops and a foundry, where the students are put to practical work as carpenters, fitters, and smiths.

Gunesh Khind, the residence of the Governor during his stay in Poona, is about five miles distant from the city. The building which cost about Rs. 10,62,278, was commenced during the tenure of office of Sir Bartle Frere, and was finished in 1871. It is in the Italian Gothic style, the main building, 300 feet in length, having a tower, which is a conspicuous object, 100 feet in height. In the south wing and centre of the building are the durbar and dining rooms, and a large conservatory.

The Empress Gardens, east of the Race Course, and the Jewish Synagogue are worth a visit, while the visitor having the time to spare should ride out of Poona and see the Parbutty Hill and temples, with the ruined palace of the Peishwa Balaji Baji Rao. Lake Fife, Kharakwasla, 11 miles distant ; Singhurh Fort, 14 miles distant and Purandhar Fort, 20 miles from Poona, are also worth visits.

There are in the station the Gymkhana, and Boat,
and Western India Clubs, four hotels, the United
Service Library, containing about 10,000 volumes, and
the Soldiers' Institute, where theatrical performances
take place. The fine Art Exhibition is held in the
Council Hall in August, the Soldiers' Industrial E hibi-
tion in the Soldiers' Institute during September, the
assault-at-arms on   taking place during
the latter month.   place about August
or September, an   he Horse and Cattle
Show, the Bom   ifle Meeting being
held during the l   October.

ior.

Note.—The address includes the name of the office to which the
telegram is to be transmitted, the name, or designation, and the
address of the addressee, and at sender's option his own name, or
designation, and his address.

TABLE OF SERVANTS' WAGES.

From 1 Rupee to 10 Rupees per Month, showing the amount per Day.

Days.	1 Re.	2 Rs.	3 Rs.	4 Rs.	5 Rs.	6 Rs.	7 Rs.	8 R.	9 Rs.	10 Rs.
	Rs.a.p.	Rs.a.p.	Rs.a.p.	Rs.a.p.	Rs.a.p.	Rs.a.p.	Rs.a.p.	Rs.a.p.	Rs.a.p.	Rs.a.p.
1	0 0 6	0 1 1	0 1 7	0 2 1	0 2 8	0 3 2	0 3 8	0 4 3	0 4 9	0 5 4
2	0 1 1	0 2 2	0 3 2	0 4 3	0 5 4	0 6 4	0 7 5	0 8 6	0 9 7	0 10 8
3	0 1 7	0 3 2	0 4 9	0 6 4	0 8 0	0 9 7	0 11 2	0 12 9	0 14 4	1 0 0
4	0 2 2	0 4 3	0 6 4	0 8 6	0 10 8	0 12 9	0 14 11	1 1 1	1 3 2	1 5 4
5	0 2 8	0 5 4	0 8 0	0 10 8	0 13 4	1 0 0	1 2 8	1 5 4	1 8 0	1 10 8
6	0 3 2	0 6 4	0 9 7	0 12 9	1 0 0	1 3 2	1 6 4	1 9 7	1 12 9	2 0 0
7	0 3 9	0 7 6	0 11 2	0 14 11	1 2 8	1 6 4	1 10 1	1 13 10	2 1 7	2 5 4
8	0 4 3	0 8 6	0 12 9	1 1 1	1 5 4	1 9 7	1 13 10	2 2 1	2 6 4	2 10 8
9	0 4 10	0 9 7	0 14 4	1 3 2	1 8 0	1 12 9	2 1 7	2 6 4	2 11 1	3 0 0
10	0 5 4	0 10 8	1 0 0	1 5 4	1 10 8	2 0 0	2 5 4	2 10 8	3 0 0	3 5 4
11	0 5 10	0 11 9	1 1 7	1 7 5	1 13 3	2 3 2	2 9 0	2 14 11	3 4 9	3 10 8
12	0 6 4	0 12 10	1 3 2	1 9 7	2 0 0	2 6 4	2 12 9	3 3 2	3 9 7	4 0 0
13	0 6 11	0 13 10	1 4 9	1 11 8	2 2 8	2 9 7	3 1 6	3 7 5	3 14 4	4 5 4
14	0 7 6	0 14 11	1 6 4	1 13 10	2 5 4	2 12 9	3 4 3	3 11 8	4 3 2	4 10 0
15	0 8 0	1 0 0	1 8 0	2 0 0	2 8 0	3 0 0	3 8 0	4 0 0	4 8 0	5 0 0
16	0 8 6	1 1 1	1 9 7	2 2 1	2 12 10	3 3 2	3 11 8	4 4 3	4 12 9	5 5 4
17	0 9 1	1 2 2	1 11 2	2 4 3	2 13 3	3 6 4	3 15 5	4 8 6	5 1 7	5 10 8
18	0 9 7	1 3 2	1 12 9	2 6 4	3 0 0	3 9 7	4 3 2	4 12 9	5 6 4	6 0 0
19	0 10 2	1 4 3	1 14 4	2 8 6	3 2 8	3 12 9	4 6 11	5 1 0	5 11 2	6 5 4
20	0 10 8	1 5 4	2 0 0	2 10 8	3 5 4	4 0 0	4 10 8	5 5 4	6 0 0	6 10 8
21	0 11 2	1 6 4	2 1 7	2 12 9	3 8 0	4 3 2	4 14 4	5 9 7	6 4 9	7 0 0
22	0 11 9	1 7 6	2 3 2	2 14 11	3 10 8	4 6 4	4 15 2	5 13 10	6 9 7	7 5 4
23	0 12 3	1 8 6	2 4 9	3 1 0	3 13 4	4 9 7	5 5 10	6 2 1	6 14 4	7 10 8
24	0 12 10	1 9 7	2 6 4	3 3 2	4 0 0	4 12 9	5 9 7	6 6 4	7 3 2	8 0 0
25	0 13 4	1 10 8	2 8 0	3 5 4	4 2 8	5 0 0	5 13 4	6 10 8	7 8 0	8 5 4
26	0 13 10	1 11 9	2 9 7	3 7 5	4 5 3	5 3 2	6 1 0	6 14 11	7 12 9	8 10 8
27	0 14 5	1 12 10	2 11 2	3 9 7	4 8 0	5 6 4	6 4 9	7 3 2	8 1 7	9 0 0
28	0 14 11	1 13 10	2 12 9	3 11 8	4 10 8	5 9 7	6 8 6	7 7 5	8 6 4	9 5 4
29	0 15 6	1 14 11	2 14 4	3 13 10	4 13 4	5 12 9	6 12 3	7 11 8	8 11 2	9 10 8
30	1 0 0	2 0 0	3 0 0	4 0 0	5 0 0	6 0 0	7 0 0	8 0 0	9 0 0	10 0 0

EXCHANGE TABLE AT 1s. 4d.

£	s.	d.	Rs. a. p.	£	s.	p.	Rs. a. p.	£	s.	d.	Rs. a. p.
0	0	0¼	0 0 3	0	5	0	3 12 0	3	0	0	45 0 0
0	0	0½	0 0 6	0	6	0	4 8 0	4	0	0	60 7 0
0	0	0¾	0 0 9	0	7	0	5 4 0	5	0	0	75 0 0
0	0	1	0 1 0	0	8	0	6 0 0	6	0	0	90 0 0
0	0	2	0 2 0	0	9	0	6 12 0	7	0	0	105 0 0
0	0	3	0 3 0	0	10	0	7 8 0	8	0	0	120 0 0
0	0	4	0 4 0	0	11	0	8 4 0	9	0	0	135 0 0
0	0	5	0 5 0	0	12	0	9 0 0	10	0	0	150 0 0
0	0	6	0 6 0	0	13	0	9 12 0	20	0	0	300 0 0
0	0	7	0 7 0	0	14	0	10 8 0	30	0	0	450 0 0
0	0	8	0 8 0	0	15	0	11 4 0	40	0	0	660 0 0
0	0	9	0 9 0	0	16	0	12 0 0	50	0	0	750 0 0
0	0	10	0 10 0	0	17	0	12 12 0	60	0	0	900 0 0
0	0	11	0 11 0	0	18	0	13 8 0	70	0	2	1,050 0 0
0	1	0	0 12 0	0	19	0	14 4 0	80	0	0	1,200 0 0
0	2	0	1 8 0	1	0	0	15 0 0	90	0	0	1,350 0 0
0	3	0	2 4 0	2	0	0	30 0 0	100	0	0	1,500 0 0
0	4	0	3 0 0